Fairey 1915–60

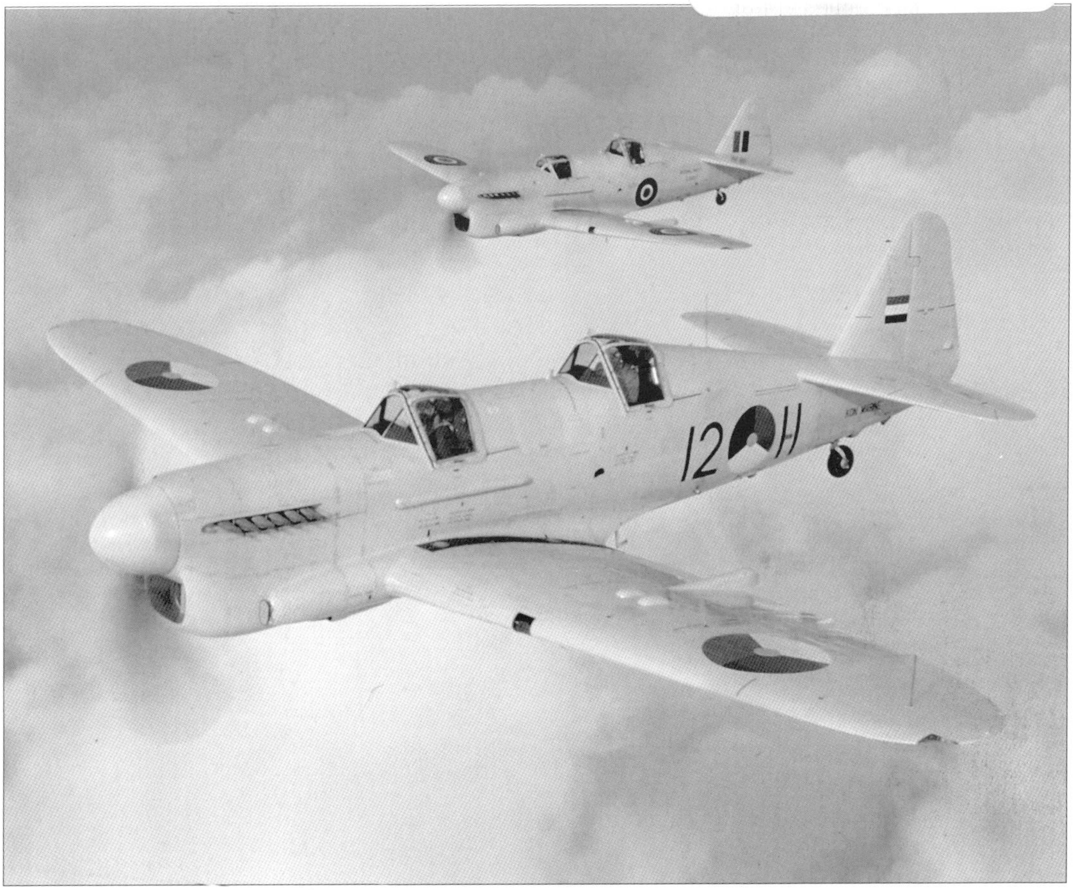

KEY Books

AVIATION INDUSTRY SERIES, VOLUME 1

Front cover image: The Royal Navy Historic Flight's (RNHF) Swordfish I, W5856; the world's oldest surviving example. (*Aeroplane*)

Back cover image: F.D.2. (*Aeroplane*)

Title page image: Fairey T.1 12-H, of the Royal Netherlands Naval Air Serve, is in the foreground alongside an example of a Royal Navy T.1, both pictured before delivery in early 1948. (Charles E. Brown via *Aeroplane*)

Contents page image: The first production Fulmar, N1854 (G-AIBE), pictured during the late 1950s, still being flown by Fairey as a company communications 'hack'. The aircraft is preserved at the FAA (Fleet Air Arm) Museum at Yeovilton. (*Aeroplane*)

Published by Key Books
An imprint of Key Publishing Ltd
PO Box 100
Stamford
Lincs
PE19 1XQ

www.keypublishing.com

Original edition published as *Fairey Company Profile 1915–1960* © 2012, edited by Martyn Chorlton

This edition © 2022

ISBN 978 1 80282 377 6

All rights reserved. Reproduction in whole or in part in any form whatsoever or by any means is strictly prohibited without the prior permission of the Publisher.

Typeset by SJmagic DESIGN SERVICES, India.

Contents

Introduction ... 4
The Fairey Story ... 5
F.16, F.17 and F.22 Campania ... 22
F.2 ... 24
N.9 ... 26
N.10 Fairey III, Seaplane and Amphibian ... 28
Hamble Baby ... 30
IIIA and IIIB ... 32
IIIC ... 34
Pintail I, II and III ... 36
IIID ... 38
Flycatcher I and II ... 40
Fawn I, II, III and IV ... 42
N.4 *Atalanta* and *Titania* ... 44
Fremantle ... 46
Fox I and IA ... 48
Ferret I, II and III ... 50
Firefly I ... 52
IIIF ... 54
Firefly II ... 56
Firefly IIIM and IV ... 58
Long-range Monoplane I and II ... 60
Fleetwing ... 62
Fox II, III, IV and V ... 64
Hendon/Night Bomber ... 66
Gordon I and II ... 68
Seal (IIIF Mk IV) ... 70
Fox VI ... 72
G.4/31 ... 74
S.9/30 and TSR.I ... 76
TSR.II and Swordfish I ... 78
Fantôme/Féroce ... 80
Fox VII and VIII ... 82
Battle ... 84
Seafox ... 86
P.4/34 ... 88
Albacore ... 90
F.C.1 ... 92
Primer Trainer ... 94
Fulmar I and II ... 96
Barracuda I ... 98
Swordfish II, III and IV ... 100
Firefly F.1 (including FR and NF.1/2) ... 102
Barracuda II ... 104
Barracuda III (aka TR.III) ... 106
Barracuda V ... 108
Spearfish ... 110
Firefly 4 and FR.4 (including F.3) ... 112
Firefly T.1, T.2, T.3, T.5 and T.7 ... 114
FB.1 Gyrodyne (aka Fairey-Bennett One) ... 116
Firefly AS/FR and NF.5 ... 118
Firefly AS.6 ... 120
Firefly TT.1, 4, 5 and 6 ... 122
Gannet (aka the Fairey 'Q', GR.17 and Fairey 17) ... 124
Firefly AS.7 and T.7 ... 126
F.D.1 (E.10/47, Type R or the Fairey Delta One) ... 128
Firefly U.8 and U.9 ... 130
Gannet AS.1 ... 132
Jet Gyrodyne ... 134
Gannet T.2 ... 136
F.D.2 ... 138
Ultra-light Helicopter ... 140
Gannet T.5 ... 142
Gannet AS.4 (including COD.4 and ECM.6) ... 144
Rotodyne ... 146
Gannet AEW.3 ... 148
Fairey Numbers ... 150
Fairey – the subcontract work ... 156

Introduction

One of the many ingredients required for creating a great aircraft company is the ability to diversify, and this was just one of the strengths that would keep the Fairey Aviation Company in business from 1915 through to 1960. Like so many other aircraft manufacturers of the day, it found its feet by taking on subcontract work, and, while this was being carried out, it began to build on its own aircraft portfolio. Fairey did not just sit back and produce aircraft in line with specifications; it designed new features that would be incorporated in all aircraft in the future.

While many companies folded during the post-World War One period, following a small order for the Fairey III, the company's future was made secure during the inter-war period. This culminated in the excellent IIIF, which was not declared obsolete until 1940!

While aircraft for the Fleet Air Arm (FAA) would be Fairey's main focus, the company branched out, briefly, into bomber design by introducing the advanced (at the time) Hendon in 1930. The Hendon was the first British cantilever heavy bomber, which, for some reason, initially missed out to the antiquated Heyford biplane bomber and was only ordered in limited numbers much later, by which time it had become obsolete.

Fairey would also achieve record-breaking success in the 1930s, when one of two long-range monoplanes built captured the long-distance record in 1933. Post-war record breaking would continue with the outstanding F.D.2, which claimed the world air speed record in March 1956.

The company's greatest, and most surprising, success story also came about in the 1930s, when the ubiquitous Swordfish, affectionately known as the 'Stringbag', entered production in 1936. By the beginning of World War Two, the Swordfish, on the surface, would appear to be completely obsolete, and by this time, its replacement, the Albacore, was already under production. But this basic torpedo-bombing biplane proved to be very effective against enemy warships during the early part of the war, achieving great success against the Italian fleet at Taranto, and crippling the *Bismarck* to such an extent, that its demise quickly followed. Later withdrawn from the torpedo role, the Swordfish achieved further success while operating from MAC ships for convoy protection duties, and by the end of the war, 21 U-boats had been claimed as sunk. This was a remarkable achievement for an aircraft that was considered by many to be completely unsuited to modern warfare, while its ultimate replacement, the Barracuda, did not achieve the same glittering war record. Post-World War Two production saw the naval theme continue with Firefly, which would see action in Korea, and finally the Gannet, which continued to serve the Royal Navy well into the 1970s.

The company's venture into rotary-wing aircraft would eventually become its undoing, despite huge technical achievements being achieved in a very short space of time. Soaked up by Westlands in 1960, the legacy of the company's final aircraft, the Rotodyne, still lives on today, and only now, in the 21st century, is the world really ready for such a fantastic machine.

The Fairey Story

The father of the company

The son of a timber merchant, Charles Richard Fairey was born on 5 May 1887, appropriately in Hendon, Middlesex, although aviation at this iconic location was still many years away. Aged only 11, Charles lost his father, who had died whilst trying to repay his creditors after, through no fault of his own, his business had failed. This not only deeply affected the whole family but also plans to send Charles to the highly respected middle-class Merchant Taylor's School at Northwood had to be shelved. Charles spent the next four years in a mainstream school instead, but, thanks to a family friend, he left school at 15 to take up employment with the Jandus Electric Company of Holloway, which specialised in producing arc lamps.

Even whilst in full employment, Charles studied four subjects five nights a week, to City and Guilds standard, in order to qualify as an electrical engineer at the Finsbury Technical College. The principal of the college was none other than Silvanus Phillips Thompson FRS, one of the country's leading electrical engineers, whose knowledge and experience would have helped Charles no end. Incredibly, he still managed to find time for one of his secret passions – building and flying model aircraft.

While gaining knowledge through his extracurricular activities, Charles was already making a name for himself at Jandus and was given responsibility for installing electric lights in the docks and warehouses at Heysham in Lancashire. Then, for some unknown reason, the rising star was sacked just a few months later, but within no time, he landed himself a reasonably well-paid job as the assistant manager and analytical chemist at Finchley power station. Already armed with a huge amount of knowledge, Charles made up his wages by lecturing at the Finchley Technical College and Tottenham Polytechnic.

By 1909, his mother had remarried, and, along with his new half-brother, Geoffrey William Hall[1], Charles and his family were able to move into a larger house. Charles was now able to spend more time on his model aircraft, which were rapidly increasing in sophistication. One of these designs was a canard monoplane with a pair of opposite-rotating pusher propellers, which neutralised the torque. He entered the model in several competitions during The Kite and Model Aeroplane Association event held on 4 June 1910. His canard model not only won the Challenge Cup but also first prize for steering, long-distance flight and stability in flight competitions. The same aircraft also won him a silver cup for the best model at The Aero Models Association on 13 August of the same year.

These model flying successes were a major turning point in Charles' life, and, seizing the moment, he penned a letter to Benjamin Varlars, the manager of the large A. W. Gamage and Co. department store in Holborn, London, who invited him to demonstrate the model. The demonstration was carried out in Hyde Park, and the subsequent deal earned Charles approximately £300 for the rights to the model, plus a royalty on every sale. Charles found a company in Balham to produce the aircraft at a cost price of 5s 6d each. Over 200 models had been delivered to A. W. Gamage by November 1910, each complete with its own case and instruction book.

---

[1] Geoffrey Hall joined Fairey in 1932 and, following service with the experimental and guided weapons department, joined the board as director of engineering in 1949. He went on to become chairman and managing director.

The prototype Fairey F.D.2, WG774, with Peter Twiss at the controls, captured en route to the 1958 SBAC show at Farnborough. (*Aeroplane*)

Up to this point, Charles' only contact with a full-size aircraft was in helping to build a monoplane for Everett Edgcumbe and Co. of Colindale in a nearby field, which was destined to become Hendon aerodrome. However, this was soon set to change when, unbeknown to him at the time, his model aircraft was found to have infringed several patents held by a Captain John William Dunne, who had been working for many years on the science of automatically stable sweptwing tailless aircraft. Dunne's company was the Blair Atholl Syndicate, which was based at Eastchurch on the Isle of Sheppey and was, at the time, owned by Sir Francis McClean and home to the Royal Aero Club. Charles offered to pay Dunne a licence fee for each model produced, but instead his only requirement was that the statement 'Licensed under J. W. Dunne's Patents' should be clearly displayed on every instruction booklet. Charles must have made quite an impression on Dunne, as Dunne offered him a job as an engineer for Blair Atholl.

Charles was now faced with a tough decision. His position at the Finchley power station was secure, while aviation during this period of time was not thought to have a serious future. His family were against the move, but Charles ignored all advice and took up the engineer's position with Dunne in 1911. This period of his life taught him a great deal about aircraft, and everyone who knew anything about flying during these early years either passed through Eastchurch or worked there in some capacity. He learned a great deal about stress calculations from Harris Booth, for example, who was working for the National Physical Laboratory. It was at Eastchurch where Charles also met three men who were destined to work for his own company in the future; Vincent Nicholl, Maurice Wright and F. G. T. Dawson. They would become a test pilot, director and financier, respectively, for Fairey in the future.

The biggest aircraft operators at Eastchurch were the Short Brothers, and Charles was most influenced by Horace Short. By late 1912, Charles was surprised to be invited to join Short Brothers as its chief stressman, a position he quickly moved on from to later become works manger and finally chief engineer. Just prior to the beginning of World War One, Short Brothers moved to its new factory on the banks of the River Medway at Rochester. This was a move that Charles was not happy about, and, along with Nicholl, Wright and Dawson, he decided to join the Royal Naval Air Service (RNAS). All but Charles were successful, so he later tried to join the Royal Flying Corps (RFC) – once again, he was unsuccessful. The excuses given for rejection were both on medical grounds and the fact that he was too valuable to lose. It was at this point that Charles Richard Fairey, aged 28, decided that it was about time he established his own aircraft manufacturing company.

Fairey Aviation Company Limited is born

Following Fairey's failures to join the RNAS and the RFC, he was told by the Director of the Air Department of the Admiralty, Commander (later Rear Admiral, Sir) Murray F. Sueter that he would be more usefully employed in designing and building aircraft. Fairey did not hesitate, and

Charles Richard Fairey (the tall man!) is pictured with friends. His prize-winning model lies at his feet.

he replied to Sueter that he would be happy to do just that, if another aircraft manufacturer would give him a subcontract. Such was the demand for aircraft at the time that, with the full approval of Horace and Oswald Short, a subcontract for a dozen Short Type 827 seaplanes was issued to Fairey to build.

Fairey now needed financial backing to establish his own company, and this was duly provided by his friend, F. G. T. Dawson, with further funds promised by Vincent Nicholl and Maurice Wright. A single room was rented at 175 Piccadilly, London, as an office and drawing room, and the company's first employee, ex-Shorts' chief draughtsman, A. C. Barlow, was taken on. With capital of £35,000, made up of 25,500 preference shares of £1 each and a further 200,000 deferred shares valued at one shilling each, the Fairey Aviation Company Limited was officially registered in July 1915, with C. R. Fairey as the only name published as the 'first director'.

The struggle now began to get the company off the ground, and Fairey was faced with the challenge of finding a factory to build the 827s, the necessary manufacturing equipment, the staff to build them, and a seaplane station to reassemble the machines and test fly them. All this had to be

The workforce of the Fairey Aviation Company pictured on the North Hyde Road.

done in a hurry if Fairey was going to show the Admiralty that he was up to the task, and, equally importantly, everything had to be in place before the company's working capital of £15,000 ran out. A suitable building was eventually found in Clayton Road, Hayes, half of which was being used by the Army Motor Lorries Company (AMLC) for reconditioning work. Conveniently, many of the AMLC workers were skilled Belgian refugees and several were made available to Fairey to help build the 827s.

With some time to spare, Fairey began production of its very first aircraft contract as a subtenant in the Clayton Road factory, and further expansion took place when a flying field was purchased at Harlington, close to the GWR railway line to Reading. A hangar was erected here for 827 assembly; this site was destined to become the main Fairey factory, which was erected along the North Hyde Road during 1917 and 1918. With regard to test flying the 827 seaplanes, a site was offered to Fairey by the Admiralty at Hamble Spit, where the Hamble River flows into Southampton Water. Workshops were erected at Hamble on 4ft-high concrete stilts, owing to the marshy ground and the fact that it flooded. A wooden slipway was also built. The site was managed by Brice G. Slater, and all of the 12 Short 827s were test flown from here by Australian-born pilot Sydney Pickles.

The contracts come in

By mid-1916, the last Short 827 had been delivered, and a further contract to build 100 Sopwith 1½ Strutters for the RNAS had been won. By October 1916, work began at the Clayton Road factory, and, to cope, the facilities at Harlington Road were expanded to include a large two-storey building for experimental and development work and to accommodate a much larger drawing office.

Fairey obviously needed more space at Clayton Road, which the AMLC were reluctant to give up. However, thanks to the company's solicitor, C. O. Crisp, control of the factory was prioritised for aircraft production rather than lorry refurbishment.

Within the space of 12 months, the 1½ Strutter contract had been completed. The last aircraft was flown out of a field at Kingsbury, west of Watling Street, in September 1917, as by this time, the Harlington field was too small. Other Strutters are believed to have been flown out of the fledgling Northolt aerodrome as well; an airfield that would witness many Fairey first flights.

Now on a roll, Fairey also received another contract to build 100 Sopwith Camels, but like so many other contracts issued towards the end of World War One, the work was cancelled before a single aircraft was built.

Early designs and the Fairey-patented camber gear

In the meantime, Fairey was beginning to find its feet with its own aircraft designs, under the firm hand of the head of the design section, F. Duncanson. The first was the F.2 twin-engined fighter, and this was followed by the more-successful Campania series of seaplanes. Both types were heavily influenced by Charles Fairey's experience of working at Short Brothers. However, Fairey's own unique innovations were incorporated into later aircraft, such as the Hamble Baby and the experimental N.9 and N.10 seaplanes.

The most significant invention to come out of the Fairey Aviation Company was the camber gear. This was effectively the first use of a flap being fitted to the trailing edge of a wing in order to increase the amount of lift available at take-off and landing. The gear was first fitted to the Hamble Baby and continued to feature on Fairey types right into the 1930s. The camber was the first of many Fairey patented designs; the patent was applied for on 19 May 1916, and it was issued the number '132,541'.

The Erecting Shop at the Clayton Road factory in 1917, pictured during the production of 100 Sopwith 1½ Strutters.

The Kennedy Giant

Not included in the main aircraft chapters is Fairey's involvement in the ambitious Kennedy Giant bomber, designed by C. J. H. Mackenzie-Kennedy. The giant 142ft-wingspan multiple-bay biplane was powered by four 200hp Salmson nine-cylinder, water-cooled radial engines that proved to be woefully underpowered for the 20,000lb-plus aircraft. The aircraft was heavily influenced by the aircraft designs of Igor Sikorsky, with whom Mackenzie-Kennedy had worked in Russia.

Fairey was involved, to a limited extent, in the design of the bomber but was mainly responsible for the Giant's construction, which had to be done in the open at Northolt because of its size. Given the serial No. 2337, the Giant was ready for test flying by Lieutenant Frank T. Courtney in late 1917. It was obvious from the start that the bomber would not fly far with the Salmson engines, but as long as it left the ground, Fairey would be paid for its work. Courtney managed to literally 'hop' the Giant off the ground, and the lack of power, combined with a lack of tailplane response, convinced him to pursue flight testing the aircraft no further. Inferior to the Handley Page O/400, the Kennedy Giant languished in the corner of Northolt aerodrome for many years before being scrapped in the early 1920s.

The Propeller Shop at Clayton Road, circa 1917, showing production of fixed-pitch, twin-blade propellers from start to finish.

Expansion

During the production of the Campania, space at the Clayton Road factory became very limited, owing to the dimensions of the large flying-boat, and, as a result, the majority of this aircraft type are believed to have gone through final assembly at the Hamble site. As mentioned earlier, the facilities at Harlington were expanded as a result of these space issues, thanks in part to a loan from the government of £20,000. Work on the expanding factory began in late 1917, and it was occupied by the spring of 1918. Part of the expansion included a 90ft-wide, 24ft-high Erecting Shop, complete with bay, machine and fitting shops.

The rapid run-down in demand after World War One hurt many aircraft manufacturers, including Fairey, which only produced 20 aircraft in 1919. The majority of these were Fairey IIICs, which were ordered for the North Russian Expeditionary Force.

Because of the lack of aircraft work, survival plans to keep the company going were quickly drawn up. One of these was to form Fairey and Charles Ltd., a motor-body manufacturer with a capital sum of £50,000, in the summer of 1919. However, the new company was destined to be short-lived, thanks to an order for 50 Fairey IIIDs, which saw the original version of the aviation manufacturer back in business in a healthy way. While it would not be in the most comfortable of positions until the late 1920s, orders for the Fawn, Flycatcher and IIIF saw the company through the rest of the decade.

With this in mind, Fairey managed to build a healthy enough bank balance to enable the company to pursue several private ventures. One of these was the risky plan to licence-build the Curtiss D-12 engine, which cost the company £20,000. The result was the excellent Fox light bomber, which only served in very limited numbers with the RAF. The Fox's design would make quite an impression on the way British aircraft were designed but would not, in the short term, benefit the company that introduced it. Fairey was also frowned upon for the way it promoted American aviation in Britain, and one high-ranking industrial leader of the day described Charles Fairey as being a 'representative of the Curtiss Company'. As a result, Charles was temporarily disillusioned with the aviation business and, for a period of time, concentrated on his other passion in life, which was designing and racing his own yachts, a sport he proved to be very successful in.

Growing in strength

The year 1929 was big for Fairey, especially with regard to its value, which was now high enough to allow outside shareholders to be approached. With assets valued at £615,486, the Fairey Aviation Company Limited was registered as a public company on 5 March 1929. The same year, the company was asked not only to vacate its original factory at Clayton Road but also Northolt Aerodrome, from which it had been flight testing aircraft since 1917. It was a blessing in disguise for the latter, as Fairey was rapidly outgrowing the hangar space allocated for its use. Northolt's replacement was a 150-acre site at Harmondsworth in Middlesex, which was bought for £15,000. From the summer of 1930, Harmondsworth became Fairey's main flight test centre and would remain so until 1944 when the site was requisitioned by the Air Ministry, despite plans to turn the airfield into another large extension of the Hayes factory. While concrete runways were built and massed expansion was carried out, the military never fully took over; instead, the airfield evolved into Heathrow Airport. Fairey was offered Heston as an alternative in early 1945, but this proved unsuitable because of air traffic control issues,

The incredible Kennedy Giant, which was so large that it was assembled out in the open at Northolt.

Fairey IIIBs provide the backdrop for this photograph, which was taken in the wing-covering end of the Erecting Shop at Clayton Road.

and it instead opted for White Waltham, which was taken over in November 1947. However, Heston continued to serve as the point of departure for newly built aircraft, following full flight testing at White Waltham. Remarkably, the compensation that Fairey was owed for the Air Ministry's requisition of Harmondsworth was not fully settled until 1964, by which time the company had already moved on from aircraft manufacturing. Harmondsworth's 'billiard table' surface made it ideal for flight testing, and the first prototype to make its maiden flight from here was the Fairey Hendon on 25 November 1930.

Enter the Swordfish, just!

Only those people who actually worked for Fairey and the many civil servants involved in the specification for the Fairey Swordfish ever knew how close the type came to being scrubbed. Luckily for Fairey, the loss of the TSR.I in September 1933 took place eight months before the company's main competitor for the specification, the Blackburn Shark, first flew. The aircraft's replacement, the TSR.II, was designed and manufactured in an incredibly short period of time. Cutting every conceivable works procedure, the components were manufactured wherever space could be found within the Hayes factory walls. In the space of seven months, the TSR.II prototype, later to be named Swordfish, was completed, but Fairey was left to wait until April 1935 for the first production order to be placed.

When another large order for the Battle was received, it was time to expand again, and, in late 1935, Fairey took over the ex-Willys-Overland Crossley car factory at Heaton Chapel in Stockport. Hayes was expanded again in October 1938 when a brand-new research department was opened by Air Minister Sir Kingsley Wood. It was the country's first private venture research centre, and the well-equipped facility included a large wind tunnel that had a test chamber 22ft long and a working section 12ft high and 10ft wide.

An example of a Felixstowe F.3, which was rebuilt by Fairey at Hamble in 1920. The aircraft is pictured at Funchal on 22 March 1921 after its first flight from Madeira to Lisbon. (Via Stuart Leslie and Martyn Chorlton)

Fairey IIIF Mk IIIs under production at Hayes, circa 1926.

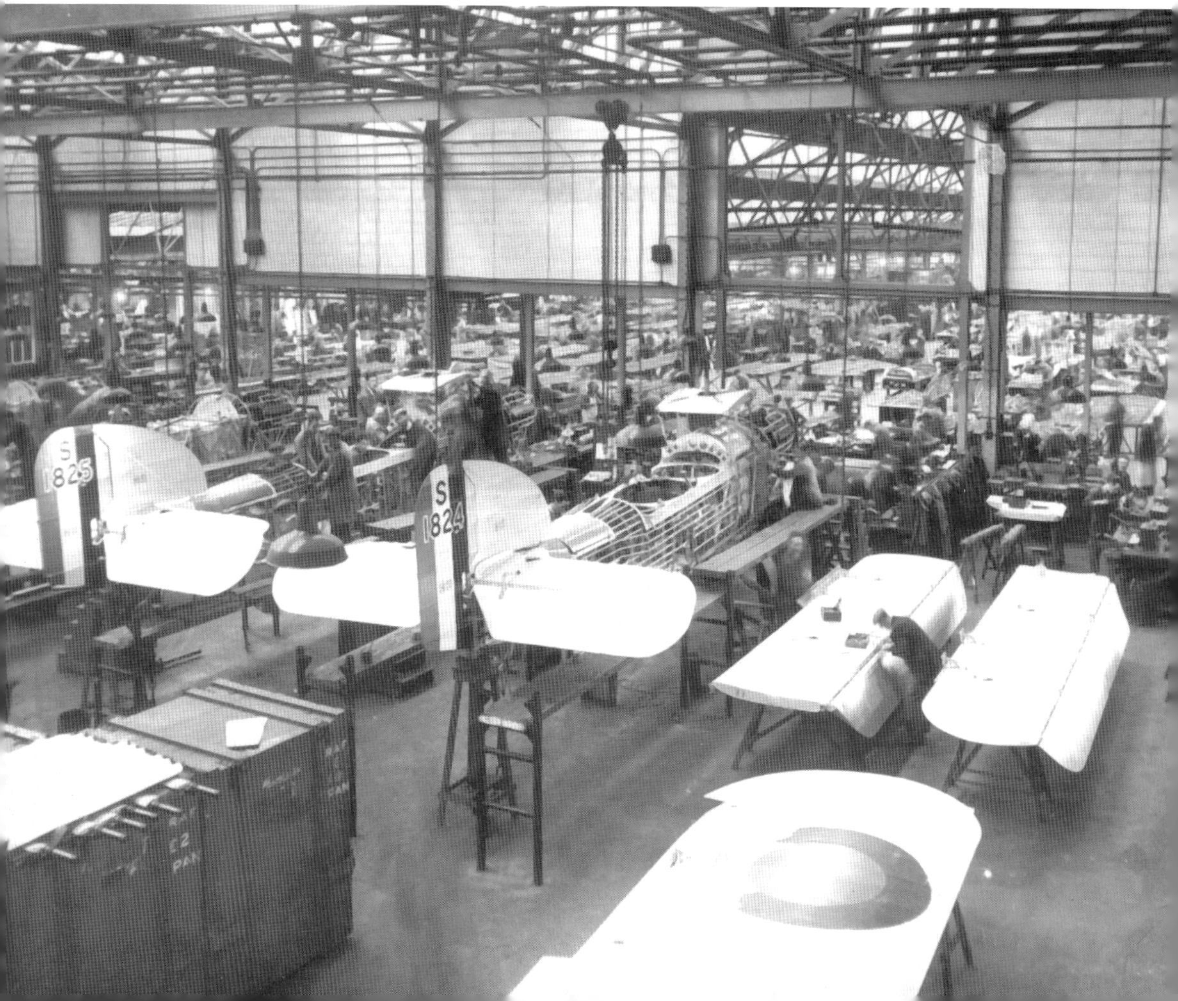

The vast Fairey 'empire'

By the beginning of World War Two, Fairey was responsible for 25 factories and workshops of its own and many more that were operated by a host of subcontractors of varying sizes. By now, the Fairey Group was not only producing aircraft but also providing spares, aircraft repair, production and repair of propellers, production of standardised components for the aviation industry as a whole, production of special machinery and experimental work across the board.

New aircraft were built at Hayes and Heaton Chapel, which had satellite factories spread across the north west. Aircraft were assembled and flight tested at Heathrow (ex-Harmondsworth) in the south and from Ringway in the north. The Swordfish, Albacore and Firefly were all built at Hayes (although Blackburn took over production of the Swordfish in 1940). At Heaton Chapel, the Battle, Fulmar and Barracuda poured out by the hundred, while a shadow factory at Errwood Park carried out the subcontract production of the Beaufighter and Halifax.

During World War Two, Charles Fairey was ordered to work for the British Air Commission in the US; an appointment he was criticised for accepting, despite having no choice at the time. However, in hindsight, Charles' work in the US was far more important than the future of his own company at the time. The problem with his departure across the pond in August 1940 was that Charles had not left anyone behind with complete control over the company, and even before this appointment, he had devoted much of his time working for the Ministry of Aircraft Production (MAP) under the control of Lord Beaverbrook.

A close up of one of the more than 600 IIIFs built by Fairey, pictured in the main Erecting Shop at Hayes during the late 1920s.

The Battle prototype pictured over Fairey's own airfield at Harmondsworth, which would later be developed into Heathrow airport.

With Charles away, Fairey's aircraft production at Hayes inevitably did not run as smoothly as hoped. For example, pending the taking over of Swordfish production by Blackburn and the frustratingly slow progress with Albacore production (in 1942, Hayes was brimming with Albacores when it should have been producing Fireflies), the Firefly was delayed by more than a year. It was a similar story at Heaton Chapel, where Barracuda production was delayed until 1942, although this was more due to the demand for the Rolls-Royce engine during the early part of the war.

A healthy post-war order book

Fairey came out of World War Two in a remarkably healthy condition with regard to aircraft production. Large orders for the Firefly, and later the Gannet, were already in place, not to mention a considerable amount of subcontract work at Heaton Chapel.

The company now looked at rotary-wing aircraft, which, in hindsight, may have been a mistake, considering the technical infancy of such machines during the post-World War Two period. Fairey's contribution to rotary-wing was very technically progressive, yet ultimately, it was also a failure.

Fairey's solution to advance the concept, was to combine the best features of the helicopter and the autogyro. This began with the unimaginatively named Gyrodyne in 1946, followed by the Jet Gyrodyne, which ultimately led to the amazing Rotodyne. In November 1955, Sir Charles Fairey chaired what was

One of Fairey's greatest, and possibly most surprising, success stories, the Fairey Swordfish. (Via *Aeroplane*)

An incredible mix of Fairey aircraft types under the same roof, including various marks of Firefly, three Spearfish prototypes and Fulmar G-AIBE, the company communications hack, in the foreground. (*Aeroplane*)

The sprawl of the main Fairey factory at Hayes, looking west, as it appeared in June 1946. (Fairey Surveys Via Martyn Chorlton)

to be his last annual general meeting. He announced that the company had still managed to achieve a profit of £2 million, despite the massive development costs that the Gannet, Gyrodyne and F.D.1 had cost Fairey. Despite this, it was obvious that a stark period lay ahead for Fairey and the aircraft industry as a whole. In April 1957, the issue of the White Paper on Defence confirmed the aircraft industry's fears by declaring that all the future costs of aircraft development should be paid for by the industry itself, rather than the government.

The future rapidly turned bleak, as the Gannet came to the end of its production run, the Rotodyne had a doubtful future, and hopes for a spin-off development supersonic fighter version of the Fairey F.D.2 came to nothing. Fairey, like so many other companies, had pinned its hope on a potential for the Operational Requirement 339, which would become the TSR.2. Even at an early stage, Fairey thought that the most likely candidates to win this work would be English Electric or Vickers-Armstrongs, but a potential merger with either was also in the offing. Another more plausible merger at the time was the rotary-wing divisions of Bristol and Westland, which did ultimately take place, but with Westland becoming the controlling company.

On 31 March 1959, Fairey Aviation Company Limited, renamed the Fairey Company Limited, became a holding company for a host of subsidiaries. The same day, Fairey Aviation Ltd was formed to nurture aircraft and manufacturing work across the country. Work being carried out by Fairey was

The imposing main headquarters building of the Fairey Aircraft Company Limited at Hayes, during the late 1940s. (Via Martyn Chorlton)

only on the Gannet and Rotodyne by this time, while operations at Heaton Chapel, now referred to as the Stockport Aviation Company, continued on limited subcontracts. The latter was then taken over by Fairey Engineering, which was secured as a subsidiary of the holding company. At the same time, the following were also created: Fairey Hydraulics, Fairey Surveys and several other non-aviation companies within Britain.

By 1960, Fairey had left the aviation industry, but, in August 1972, the opportunity arose to acquire the entire share capital of Britten-Norman aircraft based at Bembridge on the Isle of Wight. When the Fairey Aviation Group took over, Britten-Norman had 354 Islanders in the order book. This work would be shared between the Bembridge factory and Fairey SA, in Belgium, which would build the Trislander. Unfortunately, the Fairey Group as a whole hit troubled waters in 1977 and was forced into liquidation, and Fairey Britten-Norman was sold to Pilatus in 1978.

Right: The Fairey Rotodyne flight test crew after carrying out a demonstration in June 1958. From left to right; W. R. Gellatly, J. G. P. Morton, E. J. Blackburn and Blower. (Via Martyn Chorlton)

Below: The Fairey Delta 2 (F.D.2) flight test team pictured at Boscombe Down in August 1956. Test pilot Peter Twiss is standing sixth from the left, and R. G. Slade is ninth. (*Aeroplane*)

F.16, F.17 and F.22 Campania

Development
Destined to be the first Fairey aircraft to be built in quantity, this two-seat patrol seaplane was specifically designed to operate from one particular naval vessel, the purpose-built HM Seaplane Carrier *Campania*, from which the aircraft would gain its name. The ex-Cunard liner was built in 1893 and purchased by the Admiralty in October 1914. Its conversion to a seaplane carrier, with a 120ft (later modified to 200ft)-flying deck on an extended foredeck, was completed in April 1915 by Cammel Laird.

Design
An unequal-span two-bay biplane, the Campania, was made of wood with a fabric covering. The wings, with ailerons fitted to the upper, could be folded for shipboard stowage, both being hinged at the point they met the narrow fuselage. The main floats were pontoon-type, attached to the undercarriage crossbars by four bungee shock absorbers while wing tip floats were fitted directly to the underside of the outer wings. A larger tail float was also fitted, complete with a water rudder. 200 serials were allocated for Campania production, from which 100 aircraft were ordered and 62 were built. The aircraft was built in three main versions, the main difference being the powerplant.

Operational service
The prototype F.16, N1000, powered by an Eagle IV engine, made its first flight from Hamble in February 1917 in the hands of Sydney Pickles. Aircraft number two was designated as the F.17 and given the serial N1001; it was powered by a 275hp Eagle V and was effectively the second prototype. Both these aircraft later served with the RNAS, N1000 carrying out a record-breaking flight from the Isle of Grain to Scapa Flow. The pilot, Lieutenant (later Squadron Leader) Maurice E. A. Wright AFC, was destined to become a director with the Fairey Aircraft Company. The main variant was the F.22, of which 62 were built, 50 of these (N1000 to N1009 and N2360 to N2399) were built at Fairey's Hayes factory, while the remaining 12 (N1840 to N1851) were constructed by Barclay, Curle and Co., based in Clydeside. Operational service not only involved serving with the *Campania* but also the light-carriers *Nairana* and *Pegasus*. Service with the *Nairana* included duty as part of the British North Russian Expeditionary Force in 1919. Shore service saw Campanias operating with 240 and 210 TDS (Training Depot Stations) from Calshot and 241 TDS at Bembridge and Portland.

Technical data – F.16, F.17 and F.22 Campania	
ENGINE	(F.16) 250hp Rolls-Royce Mk IV (Eagle IV); (F.17) 275hp Rolls-Royce Mk I (Eagle V); (F.22) 260hp Sunbeam Maori II
WINGSPAN	61ft 7in
LENGTH	(F.16) 43ft 4in; (F.17 and F.22) 43ft 1in
HEIGHT	15ft 1in
WING AREA (total)	(F.16) 686.6 sq ft; (F.17 and F.22) 674.6 sq ft
EMPTY WEIGHT	(F.16) 3,725lb; (F.17) 3,713lb; (F.22) 3,672lb
LOADED WEIGHT	(F.16) 5,252lb; (F.17) 5,530lb; (F.22) 5,329lb
MAX SPEED (sea level)	(F.16 and F.17) 89mph; (F.22) 85mph
CLIMB (to 2,000ft)	(F.16) 5mins 20secs; (F.17) 5mins 35secs; (F.22) 7mins
SERVICE CEILING	(F.16) 7,300ft; (F.17 and F.22) 6,000ft
ENDURANCE	(F.16) 6hrs 30mins; (F.17) 5hrs; (F.22) 4hrs 30mins

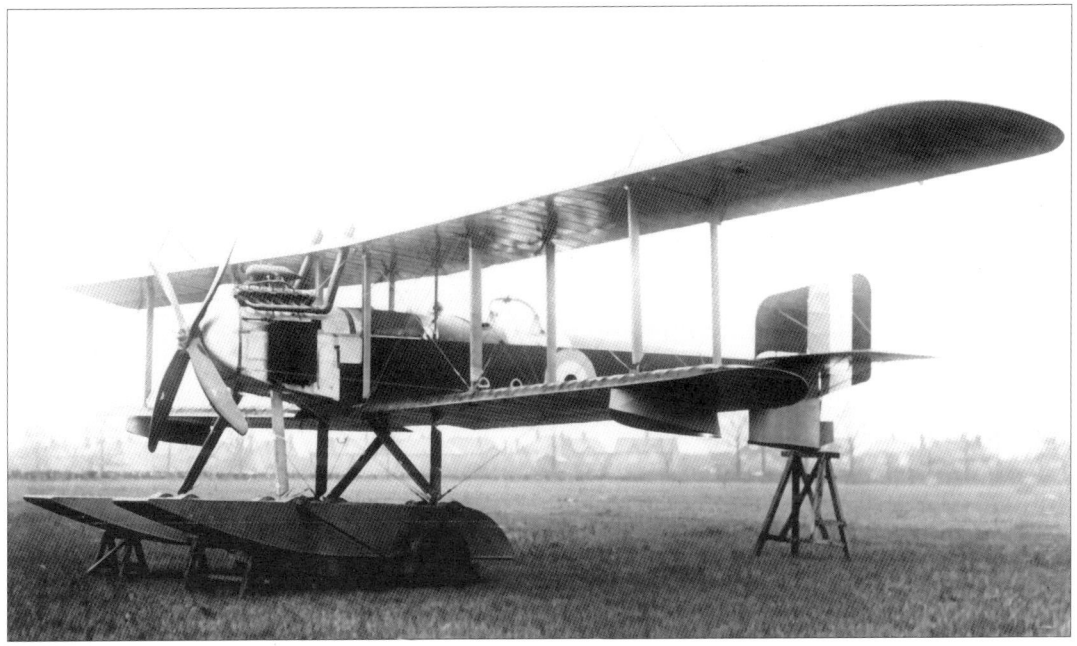

The prototype Fairey F.16 Campania, N1000, pictured at Hayes in early 1917, prior to its maiden flight on 16 February. (Via Martyn Chorlton)

F.2

Development
While the F.2 was not the first aircraft to be built by Fairey, as it had already been carrying out subcontract work building Short Type 827s and was in the process on constructing Sopwith 1½-Strutters as well, it was the first designed and built in-house. Ordered by the Admiralty, the F.2 was a large twin-engine, three-seat landplane which was intended for use as a long-range fighter, a general-purpose aircraft or even a bomber.

History and design
Design work began on the F.2 in November 1915, and, although several preliminary versions of the aircraft would also have been designed prior to the F.2 appearing in its final form, no evidence exists as to how the aircraft evolved. Three aircraft, in two versions, were initially planned and allocated the serial range No.3702 to 3705. The first version was to be tractor powered and the second pusher, while two of the aircraft were to be powered by 200hp Brotherhood Ltd engines (believed to be Green engines built under licence). Fairey planned for the three aircraft to be the F.1 (3702), F.2 (3704) and the F.3 (3705); however, neither 3702 nor 3705 reached a particularly advanced stage of design. A three-bay biplane, the F.2 was fitted with a heavy-duty four-wheel undercarriage to make night landings safer and reduce the risk of the aircraft 'nosing over'. The wings could be folded outboard of the engines, the latter being 'handed' or, in other words, opposite-rotating so as to counteract torque reaction and swing. The tailplane had twin fins and rudders. What is known about the development of the F.2 is that the engines were initially designed in tandem, buried in the fuselage driving outboard mounted propellers via a chain-and-sprocket system. This complex idea was later changed to a more conventional arrangement. The wing-mounted design and the relatively unknown Brotherhood powerplants were changed in favour of a pair of 190hp Rolls-Royce Falcon engines. It was this design that advanced to the prototype stage.

Operational service
The sole prototype was constructed in a wooden shed at Harlington, near the same site that would see the company's complex factory at Hayes completed just 18 months later. It is believed that the F.2 No.3704 first flew, albeit in very short hops, from a nearby field, in the spring of 1917. However, the first official flight was carried out by Sydney Pickles from Northolt, where it was transported by road and then reassembled on 17 May 1917. Despite the war being far from over, the Admiralty interest had by then been lost, and the day of the large, slow, multi-seat, multi-engined fighter was over. It is possible that the F.2 could have proved useful against the Zeppelin and possibly in deep-penetration operations as well.

Production
Only a single aircraft, No. 3704, was built.

F.2

Technical data – F.2	
ENGINE	Two 190hp Rolls-Royce Falcon 12-cylinder vee liquid-cooled
WINGSPAN	77ft
LENGTH	40ft 6in
HEIGHT	13ft 6in
WING AREA (total)	814 sq ft
LOADED WEIGHT	4,880lb
MAX SPEED	93mph at sea level
LANDING SPEED	38mph
CLIMB	5,000ft in 6mins
ENDURANCE	3hrs 30mins

The sole Fairey F.2 was the first aircraft to be designed and built by the fledgling Fairey Company. The giant 'fighter' is pictured outside the original Harlington 'assembly' shop, which would make way for the beginnings of the giant Fairey factory at Hayes. (Via Martyn Chorlton)

N.9

Development

It was from a pair of experimental seaplanes, unimaginatively referred to as N.9 and N.10, that the long and enduring series of Fairey III aircraft evolved. In 1916, there was a renewed enthusiasm for aircraft carrying out spotter duties for the Royal Navy, especially since the US Navy had, by this time, three cruisers fitted with catapults. This type of launching had already been studied by the Admiralty before the war began but had unwisely been put on hold. Tenders were put out for an aircraft catapult in 1916 capable of launching an aircraft weighing up to 2½ tons, propelling it at 60mph in a space of no more than 60ft and all without breaching an acceleration of 2.5g. N.9 would later be tested on a catapult and be built by another great aircraft manufacturer, Sir W. G. Armstrong Whitworth.

Design

The N.9, or F.127, was a single-bay, folding-wing biplane, the upper mainplane being of a considerably longer span, almost giving the aircraft a sesquiplane appearance. The aircraft was built to Admiralty specification N.2(a), which called for a two-seat aircraft, specifically for operations from seaplane carriers. It was destined never to be used for such a purpose, spending the bulk of its existence performing experimental work with a prototype catapult. Power was provided by a 200hp Falcon I engine, giving N.9 a maximum sea-level performance of 90mph. N.9 was also fitted with camber-changing gear and flaps along the entire length of the lower wing and between the centre-section of the upper wing, as far as the ailerons.

Operational service

N.9 first flew on 5 July 1917, and, as mentioned earlier, spent a great deal of time being used on catapult trials. Much of this was with the appropriately known catapult vessel HMS *Slinger*, which joined N.9 at the MEAD (Marine Experimental Aircraft Depot) at Grain for tests from June 1918. The trials were under the command of Lieutenant Colonel H. R. Busteed, who also carried the majority of flying in N.9. Launches were carried out from HMS *Slinger* both at anchor and under steam, and were the first of their kind to be carried out in Britain using a seaplane. Earlier trials with another catapult were carried out at Hendon using a landplane. Despite the advances being made, it would not be until October 1925 that the first service aircraft was launched from a Royal Navy warship's catapult. Purchased back from the Admiralty by Fairey in 1919, N.9 was modified with a 250hp Maori II engine and equal-span wings. It is believed that N.9 was being prepared to be an entrant for the race to carry out the first non-stop crossing of the Atlantic, a challenge for which the *Daily Mail* was offering a prize of £10,000. Instead, N.9 became one of the earliest aircraft to be civil-registered, as K-103 (the future 'G' prefix came later, all civilian aircraft were initially registered as 'K', beginning with K-100) and later G-EAAJ. By May 1920, N.9 had been sold to the Norwegian Navy, where it served until purchased by Bjorne Neilson and registered as N-20 in 1927. The long-serving aircraft suffered an irreparable accident on 12 June 1928 and was scrapped in February the following year.

Technical data – N.9	
ENGINE	One 200hp Rolls-Royce Falcon I 12-cylinder vee liquid-cooled; later one 250hp Sunbeam Maori II 12-cylinder vee liquid-cooled
WINGSPAN	50ft
LENGTH	35ft 6in
HEIGHT	13ft
WING AREA (total)	456 sq ft
EMPTY WEIGHT	2,699lb
LOADED WEIGHT	3,812lb
MAX SPEED	90mph at sea level
CLIMB	2,000ft in 4mins 10secs
ENDURANCE	5hrs 15mins
ARMAMENT	One Lewis machine-gun on a Scarff ring for observer/gunner in rear cockpit

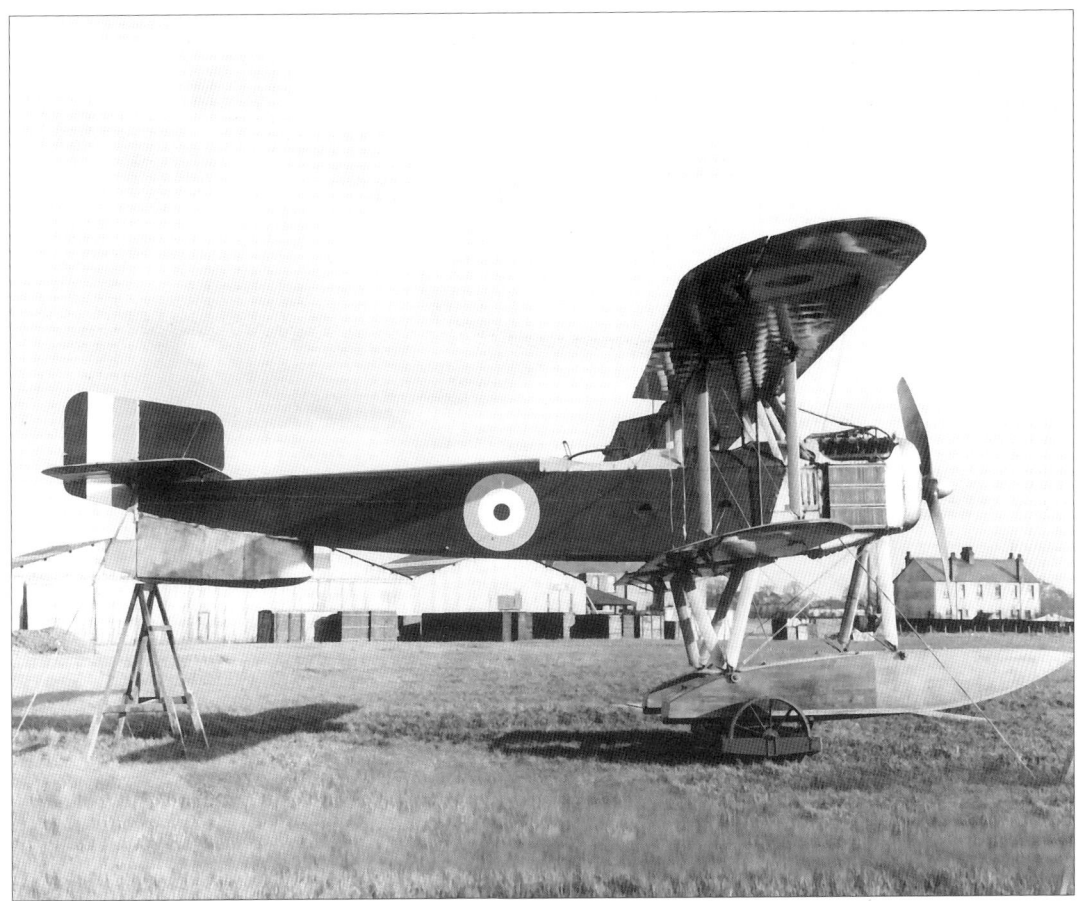

N.9 in its original form, with a Falcon I engine and large upper mainplane, pictured at Hayes before it was transferred to the Isle of Grain for trials. (Via Martyn Chorlton)

N.10 Fairey III, Seaplane and Amphibian

Development
The second of two aircraft designed to meet Admiralty specification N.2(a) was, like the N.9, only referred to by its serial N.10 and/or by the Fairey construction number, F.128. This aircraft was an alternative carrier-based seaplane designed by F. Duncanson, and it would later be designated as the Fairey III.

Design
N.10 was an equal-span two-bay biplane of slightly bigger proportions and weight than the N.9. It was fitted with folding wings and a more powerful 260hp Sunbeam Maori engine. The fuselage was the same as N.9, the only difference being a larger fin, while, like its stablemate, a full-span variable camber gear was also fitted to the lower wing and ailerons fitted to the upper. Cooling, like N.9, was via radiators mounted either side of the engine, but when N.10 was later converted to a landplane configuration, a radiator was mounted in front of the engine.

Service
N.10 was first flown on 14 September 1917, by Lieutenant Commander Vincent Nicholl, DSO, DFC from the Isle of Grain after being delivered there on 31 August. Following a host of different trials and military modifications, N.10, just like N.9, was bought back from the Admiralty by Fairey. N.10 acquired the civil registration, G-EALQ, in May 1919, and, in September it made its first public appearance at Bournemouth for the Schneider Trophy air race. Now referred to as the Fairey III, the aircraft had changed a great deal, appearing as a single-seat single-bay machine with its span reduced to 28ft and its engine replaced by a 450hp Napier Lion. While the Fairey III did not win the trophy, it was by far the most robust entrant and the only aircraft to return to its moorings under its own power at the end of the race. G-EALQ also appeared at an Air Ministry commercial aircraft competition held at Felixstowe and Martlesham Heath during August and September 1920. The Fairey III was the only floatplane to enter, and for the competition was returned to its original equal-span, two-bay biplane design, but with a two-seat, side-by-side passenger cockpit aft of the pilot. The floats, ingeniously, were combined with a retractable wheeled undercarriage, making the aircraft a useful amphibian. A total of £16,000 was for the taking at the competition, which was won by the Vickers Viking III, with the Supermarine Seagull second and the Fairey III winning £2,000 for third. G-EALQ was used by Fairey as a communications aircraft until late 1922, mainly operating from Hamble.

Technical data – N.10 Fairey III	
ENGINE	(N.10) One 260hp Sunbeam Maori II 12-cylinder vee liquid-cooled; (III) One 450hp Napier Lion 12-cylinder liquid-cooled
WINGSPAN	(N.10) 46ft 2in; (III) 28ft
LENGTH	36ft
HEIGHT	11ft 10in
WING AREA (total)	542 sq ft
EMPTY WEIGHT	(Sea) 2,970lb; (Amphibian) 3,771lb
LOADED WEIGHT	4,159lb
MAX SPEED	(Sea) 104mph at sea level; (Amphibian) 118mph at sea level
LANDING SPEED	(Amphibian) 54mph
CLIMB	2,000ft in 3mins 45secs
SERVICE CEILING	14,000ft
ENDURANCE	4hrs 30mins

N.10 (Fairey III) following its civilian registration to G-EALQ and conversion to an amphibian. (Via Martyn Chorlton)

Hamble Baby

Development
The Hamble Baby, from a design perspective, was one of the most important aircraft built by Fairey prior to the arrival of the Fox, but the aircraft originated from another manufacturer. The aircraft was a redesigned version of the Sopwith Baby, which had its roots in the 1914 Schneider Trophy-winning Tabloid. Fairey had built several Sopwith Baby floatplanes, but one particular aircraft, No.8134, arrived at the Hamble works on 23 October 1916 for repair. Fairey not only repaired the Baby but also took the opportunity to install several modifications, the most obvious being the Fairey camber changing gear.

Design
The camber gear that set the Hamble Baby apart from the original was a system of half-span trailing edge flaps that could operate in unison to increase lift or differentially to control roll or lateral movement. Prior to the introduction of the gear, the early Tabloid aircraft had a tendency to suffer float failure during take-off because of the weight demands being placed upon it. The increased lift achieved by the camber helped the Baby, and the combination of the Clerget engine gave the aircraft the capability to carry an offensive war load of two 65lb bombs and a single synchronised Lewis machine gun. Originally designed as a floatplane, a large proportion of all Babies built were landplane variants, which were designated as Hamble Baby Converts and fitted with a wide-track wheeled undercarriage.

Operational service
The Hamble Baby seaplane did not enter service until May 1918, initially joining 403 (Seaplane) Flight at Seaton Carew, 406 (Seaplane) Flight at Westgate, 412 (Seaplane) Flight at Bembridge, 450 (Baby Seaplane) Flight at Dundee, 359 (Flying Boat) Flight at Otranto and 441 (Seaplane) Flight at St Maria Di Leuca. All but 403 Flight, which only used the Hamble until August 1918, were incorporated into new RAF squadrons. 253 Squadron, formed on 7 June 1918 at Bembridge, was the first RAF squadron to receive the type, followed by 219 Squadron at Westgate in July, 229 and 249 squadrons in August and, finally, 263 Squadron at Otranto, which had incorporated both 359 and 441 Flights.

Technical data – Hamble Baby	
ENGINE	One 110hp (possibly only fitted to the first ten produced by Fairey) or 130hp Clerget rotary
WINGSPAN	27ft 9in
LENGTH	23ft 4in
HEIGHT	9ft 6in
WING AREA (total)	302 sq ft
EMPTY WEIGHT	1,386lb
LOADED WEIGHT	1,946lb
MAX SPEED	90mph at 2,000ft
CLIMB	2,000ft in 5mins 30secs
SERVICE CEILING	7,600ft
ENDURANCE	2hrs

The Hamble Baby floatplane's service career was short, and, by the end of 1918, it had been removed from both flight and squadron service. The Hamble Baby Convert served with 481 and 483 (Fighter) Flights at Andrano and also 225 Squadron, which was formed at Alimini on 1 April 1918, not to mention several RNAS training units prior to this.

Hamble Babies were generally employed on anti-submarine and attack duties, and, while being more common in British waters, the type also served across the Mediterranean, notably from the seaplane carrier, HMS *Empress*, from which two of this aircraft attacked Turkish installations in Palestine.

Production

Priced at £2,000 each (not including armament and instruments), 180 Hamble Babies were built, of which only 50 (N1320–N1339 and N1450–N1479) were built by Fairey. 130 Babies (N1190–N1219 and N1960–N2059) were built by Parnall, of which 74 (N1986–N2059) of them were built as Hamble Bay Converts.

Right: The first Hamble Baby seaplane, believed to be No.8134, pictured on the Isle of Grain in early 1917. Note the 65lb bomb under the fuselage. (Via Martyn Chorlton)

Below: N1452 displays c/n 'F.152' on the side of the fuselage and the Fairey Aviation Co. Ltd name emblazoned on the large rear float. Note also a synchronised Lewis machine gun for the pilot, breaking with the tradition of using a Vickers in this position. (Via Martyn Chorlton)

IIIA and IIIB

Development
By late 1917, the N.10, which was actually the prototype of the III series of aircraft, was converted into a landplane with a traditional V-strut undercarriage and designated as the IIIA. An order for 50 IIIA two-seat bombers for the RNAS saw the aircraft enter production only months before the service was merged with the RFC to become the RAF.

Design
Using the same Maori II engine as the N.10, the IIIA was a better performer, mainly because of the lack of drag-inducing floats. Armament was a single Lewis machine gun on a Scarff ring for the observer, while bombs could be carried on racks under the fuselage. The first IIIA, N2850, made its maiden flight in the hands of Lieutenant Colonel G. L. P. Henderson from Northolt on 6 June 1918.

The IIIB was designed for bombing duties in response to Admiralty N.2(b) requirements, and while the fuselage was the same as the IIIA, the wing, fin and rudder were of a greater area, and the floats were larger than the N.10's. The wings folded, and the upper had a visible overhang where the ailerons were attached. These extended wing tips were braced by large kingposts directly above the inter-aircraft struts. The aircraft also employed the same camber changing gear as the Hamble Baby.

Armament was the same as the IIIA, although a bomb load of up to 600lb could be carried in tubular containers under the fuselage. Vincent Nicholl made the first flight of a IIIB, N2246, from Hamble on 8 August 1918.

Operational service
Intended as a replacement for the Sopwith 1½ Strutter, by the time the first IIIAs were due to enter service, World War One had come to an end, and, by 1919, the type had already been declared obsolete. The IIIA did join 258 Squadron at Luce Bay and 272 Squadron at Machrihanish in November 1918, but, by March 1919, both units had been disbanded. With regard to the IIIB, only 25 were built, because Fairey had the foresight to convert those on order into IIICs.

Technical data – IIIA and IIIB	
ENGINE	One 260hp Sunbeam Maori II 12-cylinder vee liquid cooled
WINGSPAN	(IIIA) 46ft 2in; (IIIB) 62ft 9in
LENGTH	(IIIA) 31ft; (IIIB) 37ft 1in
HEIGHT	(IIIA) 10ft 8in; (IIIB) 14ft
WING AREA (total)	(IIIA) 542 sq ft; (IIIB) 616 sq ft
EMPTY WEIGHT	(IIIA) 2,532lb; (IIIB) 3,258lb
LOADED WEIGHT	(IIIA) 3,694lb; (IIIB) 4,892lb
MAX SPEED	(IIIA) 109mph at sea level; (IIIB) 95mph at 2,000ft
CLIMB	(IIIA) 5,000ft in 7mins 5secs; (IIIB) 2,000ft in 4mins 10secs
SERVICE CEILING	(IIIA) 15,000ft; (IIIB) 10,300ft
ENDURANCE	(IIIA and IIIB) 4hrs 30mins

The IIIB only served with two RAF units, namely 219 Squadron at Westgate and 230 Squadron at Felixstowe from October 1918; the latter until March 1919. The IIIB saw out its days with 219 Squadron until the unit was disbanded on 7 February 1920.

Production

Fifty IIIAs were built, from N2850 to N2899. Sixty IIIBs were ordered, but this was reduced to just 25 in the serial range N2230 to N2254.

The second production Fairey IIIA, N2851 (c/n F.221). (Via Martyn Chorlton)

The prototype IIIB seaplane during flight trials at Grain in 1918. Note the extended upper wing and the additional bracing provided by the large king-posts. (Via Martyn Chorlton)

IIIC

Development
Combining the ability to bomb, as per the IIIB, and the capability to be used in the reconnaissance role, as per the IIIA, the IIIC was one of the best seaplanes designed during World War One. Unfortunately, the aircraft arrived too late to see action, entering service in November 1918.

Design
The IIIC combined the main features of its two predecessors, having the tail and equal-span wings of the III and IIIA, and the seaplane floats of the IIIB. It was the engine, an Eagle VIII, which made the biggest difference to the performance of the IIIC. Not only did the Eagle have an excellent power-to-weight ratio, but the engine was also reliable. The additional power meant that much larger fuel tanks could be installed, with a capacity of 120 gallons, which, potentially, gave the IIIC an endurance of approximately 5½ hours. Armament was a single synchronised forward-firing Vickers machine gun for the pilot and a Scarff ring-mounted Lewis for the observer. Bombs could be carried on under fuselage racks.

Operational service
The first Fairey IIIC, N2255, was flown for the first time from Hamble by Vincent Nicholl in July 1918. However, it was not until September 1918 that the first IIIC arrived at the MEAD on the Isle of Grain for testing. By November, the type had entered service with 229 Squadron at Great Yarmouth and 230 Squadron at Felixstowe, just missing out on seeing active service during World War One. Both units dispensed with their IIICs in March 1919.

The IIIC did see action in 1919 when at least seven aircraft were embarked on HMS *Pegasus* as part of the North Russian Expeditionary Force based at Archangel. Several IIICs unsuccessfully took part in an attack on four Russian naval vessels in June, although better results were achieved during a second raid on rail targets. Flight Lieutenant L. Massey Hilton, who was destined to become a director at Fairey, was awarded the DFC for his actions during this short campaign.

Production
Thirty-six Fairey IIICs were built, N2246, N2255 to N2259 and N9230 to N9259. Four IIICs joined the civilian registry; N9253 became G-EBDI, N2876 became G-EADZ (later G-EAMY), N2255 became G-EAPV and N9256 became G-EARS. The latter was later shipped to Canada via the Aircraft Disposal Co. and re-registered as G-CYCF.

Technical data – IIIC	
ENGINE	One 375hp Rolls-Royce Eagle VIII
WINGSPAN	46ft 1in
LENGTH	36ft
HEIGHT	12ft 2in
WING AREA (total)	542 sq ft
EMPTY WEIGHT	3,392lb
LOADED WEIGHT	4,800lb
MAX SPEED	110.5mph at 2,000ft
CLIMB	6,500ft in 9mins 30secs
SERVICE CEILING	15,000ft
ENDURANCE	5hrs 30mins

Originally a IIIB, N2255 (c/n F.302) became the first IIIC and was first flown by Vincent Nicholl in July 1918. Later sold on to the civilian market as G-EAPV, the aircraft is pictured at the MEAD at Grain in 1918. (*Aeroplane*)

Pintail I, II and III

Development
The Pintail was a fighter-reconnaissance seaplane designed to Specification XXI, issued on 20 May 1919 for a two-seat amphibian that could operate from land, water or an aircraft carrier. Three prototypes were built, designated from Mk I to III, each only being differentiated by varying amphibious gear and fuselage lengths.

Design
Originally named the Type XXI, after the specification, the Pintail made its first public appearance at the Olympia exhibition in July 1920. Powered by a 475hp Napier Lion V, the aircraft was designed for a crew of two and was armed with a forward fixed Vickers gun, operated by the pilot, and a Lewis gun mounted on a Scarff ring for the observer. The fuselage was made up in three parts, consisting of the powerplant, a centre-section made of steel that carried the wings and undercarriage, and the rear fuselage, which included the rear cockpit. Both the front and rear sections of the fuselage could be removed from the central unit for major servicing, repair or for ease of transportation.

Service
Pintail I, N133, first flew on 7 July 1920 in the hands of Vincent Nicholl and was originally fitted with amphibious gear that enabled the wheels to be retracted into the floats. Prone to letting in water, the gear was redesigned so that the wheels were mounted on a swinging frame between the floats, as per Fairey III N.10. The second Pintail, Mk II N134, first took to the air from Hamble on 25 May 1921, again by Nicholl, although freelance test pilot Norman Macmillan is credited with carrying out the type's flight test programme. The Mk II had a longer fuselage, and the wheels were, this time, fitted outboard of the floats. The amphibious gear was the main difference introduced by Pintail III, N135, which was once again first flown by Nicholl, on 8 November 1921. N135 had its main wheels fixed into the floats, protruding just enough to enable land operations and faired sufficiently in not disrupting landing on water. The Pintail was never adopted by the FAA or RAF, and a small export order of three Pintail IVs from Japan in August 1923 was the type's only success. The Mk IV had its upper wing raised by 9in, an issue with the original aircraft, and the first was delivered to the Imperial Japanese Navy in August 1924.

Production
Six aircraft, one Mk I, II and III (N133–N135) and three Mk IVs (F.478–F.180) were built.

Technical data – Pintail I, II and III	
ENGINE	One 475hp Napier Lion V 12-cylinder, broad-arrow, liquid-cooled
WINGSPAN	40ft; (folded) 15ft 8in
LENGTH	32ft 3in
HEIGHT	11ft
WING AREA	400 sq ft
LOADED WEIGHT	4,700lb
MAX SPEED	125mph at 2,000ft
CLIMB	5,000ft in 5mins 8secs
SERVICE CEILING	15,000ft
ENDURANCE	5hrs 30mins

N135, the Pintail III, first flew on 8 November 1921. It is pictured at Hamble before it was delivered to the MAEU at Grain in December 1921. (Via Martyn Chorlton)

IIID

Development

The IIID ranks as one of the most successful aircraft ever produced by Fairey. This straightforward, robust and reliable aircraft was a common sight during the 1920s, serving in larger numbers with the FAA and RAF, as well as achieving several export orders. Built to Air Ministry Specification 38/22, production continued from 1921 to 1925, by which time 207 IIIDs had been delivered to the FAA and RAF, collectively. The IIID's greatest strength was its incredible versatility, being able to operate as a landplane from aircraft carriers or shore bases. It could also be launched from a catapult on a warship as a seaplane, and be operated as a general-purpose aircraft, bomber or spotter-reconnaissance with either wheels or floats.

Design

The IIID was a folding, equal-span, two-bay biplane made of wood and incorporated several new design features over its predecessor, the IIIC. One of these features was an oleo-pneumatic undercarriage, making the IID the first landplane to use such a system. Another novel feature was that the entire forward fuselage, including the engine and its steel bearers, could be removed as a single separate unit. In FAA service, the IIID was generally fitted out as a three-seater on floats, although seven were built as trainers or target-tugs in a two-seat configuration with dual-controls. General-purpose variants were armed with a forward fixed Vickers machine gun, a Scarff ring mounted Lewis in the rear and a bomb load of up to 400lb.

Technical data – IIID seaplane, landplane and transatlantic load carrier (TLC)	
ENGINE	One 365hp Rolls-Royce Eagle VIII and IX 12-cylinder vee liquid-cooled; One 450hp Napier Lion II/IIB/V and VA 12-cylinder broad-arrow liquid-cooled
WINGSPAN	46ft 1¼in; (TLC) 62ft
LENGTH	(Sea and TLC) 36ft 1in; (Land) 31ft 5in
HEIGHT	(Sea) 13ft; (Land) 12ft
WING AREA (total)	500 sq ft
EMPTY WEIGHT (equipped)	(Sea) 3,990lb; (Land) 3,430lb
LOADED WEIGHT	(Sea and Land) 5,050lb; (TLC) 7,250lb
MAX SPEED	(Sea [Lion IIB]) 117mph; (Sea [Eagle IX]) 101mph; (Land [Lion IIB]) 120mph; (Land [Eagle IX]) 110mph; (TLC) 95mph
CLIMB	(Sea [Lion IIB]) 10,000ft in 12mins 30secs; (Sea [Eagle IX]) 10,000ft in 25mins; (Land [Lion IIB]) 5,000ft in 4mins 50secs; (Land [Eagle IX]) 5,000ft in 10mins; (TLC) 350 ft/min
SERVICE CEILING	(Sea [Lion IIB]) 19,500ft; (Sea and Land [Eagle IX]) 16,500ft; (Land [Lion IIB]) 20,000ft
ENDURANCE	(Sea) 6hrs 30mins; (Land) 6hrs
RANGE	(TLC) 1,500 miles

Operational service

The prototype IIID seaplane, N9450, was first flown by Vincent Nicholl from Hamble in August 1920, who, one year later, also first flew the landplane version. A batch of 50 was initially ordered by the Air Ministry (N9450–N9499), all powered by the Eagle VIII engine. An order for 50 more followed not long after, and then another for 12 (N9657–N9578) for the RAF, powered by the 450hp Napier Lion II. 441 and 444 Flights were the first units to receive the IIID in 1924, the same year in which the RAF's carrier-based branch became the FAA. It was with the RAF that the IIID achieved national fame, when the first official long-distance formation flight was formed at Northolt in November 1925. The Cape Flight, led by Wing Commander C. W. H. Pulford, set out in IIID S1102–S1105 on 1 March 1926 from Heliopolis, bound for Cape Town. On 19 April, all four IIIDs arrived safely in South Africa before beginning the long flight back to England. The quartet staged back through Greece, Italy and France, arriving at Lee-on-Solent (floats had been fitted at Aboukir) on 21 June 1926, having completed a remarkable flight of 13,901 miles without a single mechanical failure or incident.

Production

There were 207 built for the FAA and RAF and 20 built for export to Australia, Portugal and the Netherlands.

Fairey IIID Mk II N9575, one of a batch of 12 aircraft ordered in February 1923 to Contract No.375547/22. The aircraft is pictured over a cloud-covered Malta during its service with 481 Flight, based at Kalafrana. (Via Martyn Chorlton)

Originally built for service with the Cape Flight, IIID Mk III S1108 is pictured during its service with 445 Flight, HMS *Resolution*, over the Mediterranean. (Via Martyn Chorlton)

Flycatcher I and II

Development
The Flycatcher had a typical naval aircraft design that sacrificed its appearance for performance, yet despite this, the small, traditional fighter looked the part, and, from its introduction in 1923, loyally served the FAA into the mid-1930s.

Design
Designed and built to Air Ministry Specification 6/22 (which was looking for a deck-landing single-seat fighter to replace the Nightjar), the prototype Flycatcher, N163, was first flown from Hamble by Vincent Nicholl on 28 November 1922. The Flycatcher could operate as a fighter with a standard undercarriage, or be fitted with amphibious landing gear (floats with an integrated wheel protruding by a few inches). The latter option allowed the Flycatcher to land and take off with the floats still in place. General construction of the fuselage was of wood and metal, while the wings were solely made of wood with all surfaces covered in fabric. Not the most attractive of aircraft, the Flycatcher had single-bay staggered wings, the upper having a dihedral of five degrees, while the fuselage gave the impression of curving upwards towards the squared-off tail unit. Complete with camber gear installed, the Flycatcher was very popular with its pilots and ground crew alike. Easy to fly, very manoeuvrable, the Flycatcher could do no wrong.

The Flycatcher II, of which only one aircraft, N126, was built, first flew on 3 October 1926. Resembling the Firefly I more than its namesake, the aircraft was designed to Specification N.21/26 for a new deck-landing fighter for the FAA. Written off in an accident in May 1929, none of the aircraft entered for the new specification was accepted by the Air Ministry.

Operational service
From its entry into service, the Flycatcher was the FAA's only standard fighter until the Hawker Nimrod arrived in 1932. It served on every Royal Navy aircraft carrier in land and floatplane configuration,

Technical data – Flycatcher I, Landplane and Seaplane I and II	
ENGINE	(I) One 400hp Jaguar II/IV or Jupiter IV; (II) 540hp Jaguar VIII (supercharged) or 480hp Mercury IIA
WINGSPAN	(I Land and Sea) 29ft; (II) 35ft
LENGTH	(I Land) 23ft; (I Sea) 29ft; (II Land) 24ft 9in; (II Float) 28ft 9in
HEIGHT	(I Land) 12ft; (I Sea/Amphibian) 13ft 4in; (II Land) 10ft 9in; (II Float) 12ft
WING AREA	(All) 288 sq ft
EMPTY WEIGHT	(I Land) 2,038lb; (I Sea) 2,571lb
LOADED WEIGHT	(I Land) 3,028lb; (I Sea) 3,531lb; (II Land) 3,266lb; (II Float) 3,667lb
MAX SPEED	(I Land) 134mph at sea level; (I Sea) 130mph at sea level; (II Land) 153mph; (II Float) 144mph
CLIMB	(I Land) 5,000ft in 3mins 41secs; (I Sea) 5,000ft in 7mins 15secs
SERVICE CEILING	(I Land) 20,600ft; (I Sea) 14,000ft
ENDURANCE	(I Land and Sea) 1hr 49mins 12secs at max speed at 10,000ft

shore bases, platforms from turrets of capital ships and from the foredecks of HMS *Courageous, Furious* and *Glorious*. 402 Flight was the first unit to receive the Flycatcher at Leuchars in April 1923, before embarking on HMS *Eagle*. By September 1924, every FAA fighter flight had re-equipped with the Flycatcher, including a pair of new flights, and, at the type's peak of service in 1930, the fighter was the only type on the strength of eight flights.

It was not until 1934 that the Flycatcher was superseded by the Hawker Osprey and Nimrod. The former replaced the Fairey fighter on catapult flights on warships. Five Flycatchers, which were operated by 403 Flight on the China Station as part of the 5th Cruiser Squadron and 406 Flight with the East Indies Squadron, were the last to see service when they were replaced by Ospreys in June 1934.

Production

195 Flycatchers were built between 1922 and 1930, including four prototypes, N163–N165 and N216, followed by production batches, serialled N9611–N9619, N9655–N9680, N9854–N9895, N9902–N9965, S1060–S1073, S1273–S1297, S1409–S1418 and S1590.

For almost two decades, a replica of a Fairey Flycatcher (S1287) graced our skies, until it was delivered to the FAA Museum at Yeovilton by John Fairey on 5 June 1996. (*Aeroplane*)

A Fairey Flycatcher takes off from the main flying deck of the aircraft carrier HMS *Glorious*, not long after the vessel was commissioned in 1930. (*Aeroplane*)

Fawn I, II, III and IV

Development
The Fawn was one of only a handful of new aircraft to enter RAF service during the austere and financially difficult 1920s. Many squadrons were still operating aircraft from World War One, so the arrival of the Fawn, which was the first of its kind to enter RAF service following the armistice, was something of anomaly.

Design
The Fawn was effectively the landplane development of the Pintail, which was originally designed as an Army co-operation and/or reconnaissance machine. Designed to Air Ministry Specification 5/21, the prototype, Fawn I, J6907, was first flown by Vincent Nicholl in March 1923. A two-seater, the Fawn was armed with a single forward-firing Vickers machine gun and up to two Lewis machine-guns on the obligatory Scarff ring in the rear. A bombload of up to 450lbs, made up of four 112lb bombs or two 230lb bombs, could be carried on under-wing racks.

The prototype had the same short fuselage as the Pintail, but a pair of follow-up prototypes, designated as Mk IIs and serialled J6908 and J6909, had longer fuselages and better longitudinal stability. It was this mark, which first flew in September 1923, that was chosen for production.

An order for 40 Mk IIs was placed by the Air Ministry to Specification 20/23, and the first production Fawn, J7182, first flew from Northolt on 29 January 1924. Once these had been built, a follow-up order for 15 Mk IIIs was issued to Specification 1/25. This mark differed in having a 468hp Lion V engine. Another engine change resulted in the Fawn IV, although only six of the Lion VI-powered variants were ordered.

Operational service
The Fawn entered service with 12 Squadron at Andover in March 1924, replacing its ageing DH.9As. 11 Squadron followed in April at Bircham Newton, with 100 Squadron at Eastchurch being the only other 'full-time' unit to fly the type. The highlight of the Fawn's service career was performing at the 1925 and 1926 Hendon Air Displays as a 36-strong massed formation. Squadrons 12 and 100 took part in both events.

Technical data – Fawn I, II and III	
ENGINE	(II) One 470hp Napier Lion II 12-cylinder broad-arrow liquid-cooled engine; (III) One 468hp Napier Lion V; (IV) One 520hp Lion VI
WINGSPAN	49ft 11in
LENGTH	32ft 1in
HEIGHT	11ft 11in
WING AREA (total)	550 sq ft
LOADED WEIGHT	5,834lb
MAX SPEED	114mph
CLIMB	5,000ft in 6mins 30secs
SERVICE CEILING	13,850ft
ABSOLUTE CEILING	15,500ft
RANGE	650 miles
ENDURANCE	5hrs

By late 1926, the Fawn was already being earmarked for replacement by the Horsley, and, in 12 Squadron's case, the Fairey Fox. The Fawn continued to serve with fledgling auxiliary 'part-time' units of 503 (City of Lincoln) Squadron at Waddington from October 1926, and 602 (City of Glasgow) Squadron at Renfrew from September 1927. It was with the latter that the type was retired in October 1929.

Production

75 Fawns were built including six prototypes in the serial ranges: Mk I, J6907; Mk II, J6908, J6909, J7182–J7231; Mk III, J7768–J7779 and J7978–J7985; Mk IV, J7215, J7768, J7773, J7780 and J7781.

The prototype Fawn, J6907, first flew on 8 March 1923. The aircraft was later converted into a Mk III and was fitted with an experimental Lioness engine (a Lion modified to run inverted). (*Aeroplane*)

Not the most attractive of Fairey designs, the Fawn's appearance was not improved by the 'official requirement' for a pair of externally mounted fuel tanks on the upper wing. (*Aeroplane*)

N.4 *Atalanta* and *Titania*

Development
In late 1917, the Admiralty issued Specification N.4 for a very large flying-boat for fleet co-operation and open-sea reconnaissance duties. The RNAS was already heavily reliant on large flying-boats for its open-sea operations, and more than 200, the majority of them Felixstowe designs, were in service by the beginning of 1918. Despite having no previous experience of building large flying-boats, especially 'very large' ones, Fairey won an order for three aircraft, two of them to be constructed by Fairey and one by the Phoenix Dynamo Manufacturing Co. of Bradford.

Design
The management and design of the Fairey N.4 was controlled from Hayes, but, even as the project was about to begin, Fairey had to subcontract one of its flying-boats to Dick Kerr and Co., at Lytham St Annes, because of a lack of floor space. The hull of the N.4 was a Linton Hope design, and these were constructed separately by boatbuilders; one by May, Harden and May, one by the Gosport Aviation Co. and the other by Fyfes on the Clyde. The project was rapidly spreading itself around the country, with six major companies involved, none of them located near each other, and this was destined to cause a great many logistical problems.

The N.4 was the largest flying-boat in the world at the time, the giant having a gross weight of over 30,000lbs. However, when the Armistice came and went, the problems of scattered production, assembly and transportation saw the project slow to a snail's pace, and the first aircraft, N119, named *Atalanta*, did not take to the air until the summer of 1923. The second aircraft, and the only other to fly, was N129 *Titania* in 1925.

The N.4 was an unequal-span biplane powered by four Condor engines, which were arranged, un-cowled, as tractor and pusher in joined pairs. The tailplane, which had three fins and rudders, was a biplane arrangement. Two pilots were accommodated in an open cockpit, and positions for gunners in the nose and two apertures behind the main plane were also provided.

Service
N119 *Atalanta*, following its assembly at Lytham in 1919, was not dismantled until 1921, after which it was transported by road to Grain. Reassembled, the giant flying-boat made its maiden flight on 4 July 1923 and, after initial flight testing, was later transferred in early 1924 to Felixstowe for further trials with the Marine Aircraft Experimental Establishment (MAEE).

The second N.4, N129 *Titania*, was assembled at Hamble, once the hull, built in Scotland, and the superstructure, built at Hayes, arrived in late 1921. Further modifications to the hull were needed, and these were carried out at Hayes, the hull later returning to Hamble where N129 resided until 1923. Dismantled, the flying boat was moved to Grain, but the first flight did not take place until 24 July 1925 following another move to Felixstowe in June 1924. *Titania* is believed to have been operated solely by the MAEE until early 1929. The third N.4, serialled N118 and named *Atalanta II*, was finally assembled at the Phoenix works in Bradford. Destined never to fly, N118 was later dismantled and transported to Grain, where the hull was used for floatation testing.

Technical data – N.4	
ENGINE	(*Atalanta*) Four 650hp Rolls-Royce Condor IA; (*Titania*) Four 650hp Condor III
WINGSPAN	139ft
LENGTH	66ft
WING AREA (total)	2,900 sq ft
LOADED WEIGHT	(*Atalanta*) 30,500lb; (*Titania*) 31,612lb
MAX SPEED	115mph at sea level
CLIMB	5,000ft in 8mins
SERVICE CEILING	14,100ft
ENDURANCE	(normal) 7hrs; (maximum) 9hrs

The first of three N.4 flying boats, although only two ever flew, was N119 (c/n F.276) *Atalanta*, pictured at Felixstowe in 1924. (Via Martyn Chorlton)

Fremantle

Development
One of many aircraft ordered for 'one-off' production by the Air Ministry, the Fremantle came about from Specification 44/22 (the last of 1922) for a long-range reconnaissance aircraft. The specification failed to mention that the Fremantle was actually ordered for an attempt to be the first aircraft to circumnavigate the world. It was intended to be piloted by Captain R. H. McIntosh of Handley Page Transport and navigated by Captain F. Tymms, the latter serving with the Civil Aviation Department of the Air Ministry, an organisation that had great influence on the specification.

Design
The Fremantle was powered by a Condor III engine fitted with spur reduction gear, which could raise the propeller hub, therefore giving the fixed-pitch wooden propeller greater tip clearance above the water. The clearance enabled the designer to incorporate shorter struts between the fuselage and the floats, which had the knock-on effect of improving aerodynamics and, in turn, improving performance. The fuselage had a large internal cabin for the crew with large side windows, and this was created using mahogany planking rather than obstructive crossed bracing. The cabin was large enough to enable crew to stand upright and was long enough to sleep in, had room for food and water storage and a navigator's table.

The pilot's cockpit was aft of the all-metal engine bay, with the added protection of a fireproof bulkhead. The pilot had a good, unobstructed view, aided by the two-bay biplane wings having a dihedral but no stagger. Good directional stability was provided by a large fixed fin and a big air-balanced rudder, which gave outstanding control in the yaw. Aided by Fairey's flap gear, and combined with an RAF 15 aerofoil, take-offs and landings were a delight. The Fremantle was fitted with five floats; the two main ones were constructed from mahogany planking for extra strength and to overcome the effects suffered by plywood floats in humid and hot conditions.

Service
By the time the Fremantle was ready for its first flight in November 1924, the round-the-world had already been achieved by a trio of US Douglas World Cruisers. The Fremantle was first flown on 28 November 1924 by Norman Macmillan, who carried out flight testing, although this did not include a period with the MAEE at Felixstowe, until 16 June 1925. During this period, Macmillan flew the aircraft for 11hrs 55mins and described the it as, 'a very pleasant aircraft to handle, both on the water and in the air'.

Serialled as N173, the Fremantle joined the MAEE in November 1925 and remained until January 1926 when it was transferred to the RAE at Farnborough for radio-navigation development work (presumably converted to a landplane). During 1925, the Fremantle was briefly registered as G-EBLZ for The Air Council, a registration it would have displayed if it had made the round-the-world attempt.

Technical data – Fremantle

ENGINE	One 650hp Rolls-Royce Condor III 12-cylinder vee liquid-cooled
WINGSPAN	69ft 2in
LENGTH	53ft
HEIGHT	20ft 3in
WING AREA	1,095 sq ft
LOADED WEIGHT	12,550lb
MAX SPEED	108mph
CLIMB	5,000ft in 25mins

Above and below: The Fremantle was one of the largest single-engine floatplanes ever built and was originally intended for an attempt on the round-the-world record, which fell to the United States eight weeks before the Fairey aircraft made its maiden flight. (Via Martyn Chorlton)

Fox I and IA

Development
It seemed to be an entrenched tradition by the mid-1920s that bombers were slow, lumbering machines while fighters were nimble and fast. The illusion was impressively shattered when Fairey introduced its outstanding Fox in 1925, an aircraft that neither looked nor performed like any other in the RAF inventory, yet it was being presented as a bomber. At 50mph faster than the Fawn, the Fox was more than capable of outpacing the in-service fighters across the world, not just the RAF's. Yet, it was the financial constraints of the period that forced a restricted order of just 28 aircraft, and only one squadron received the type. The virtually forgotten Fox certainly raised the performance bar for bombers many years before the highly credited Hawker Hart.

Design
The main reason for the Fox's excellent performance was its streamlined shape and clean lines, which were attributed to the novel use of an American powerplant. Charles Fairey was on a visit to the US in 1923 when the Curtiss D-12 engine caught his eye. The engine had a low frontal area and could be cowled very smoothly. Fairey managed to acquire the engine for his new Fox, which was not only aerodynamic around the engine but also across the entire airframe.

Operational service
The prototype Fox, only referred to by its construction number (c/n) F.573, first flew on 3 January 1925. By August, the aircraft was displayed to Air Chief Marshal Sir Hugh Trenchard, the Chief of Air Staff, who was so impressed he ordered enough Foxes to equip an entire squadron without delay. The first production Fox flew on 10 December 1925. By June 1926, the type entered service with 12 Squadron, under the command of Squadron Leader Gray, at Andover, replacing the squadron's Fawns. The squadron was destined to operate the Fox until these were replaced by the Hart in January 1931.

The Fox made a huge impression on the pilots of 12 Squadron, and other units looked on with envy as they were usually outperformed and outmanoeuvred during air exercises. From this period onwards, 12 Squadron rebadged itself with the head of a fox and the motto 'Leads the Field'. The Fairey Fox certainly did.

Technical data – Fox I and IA	
ENGINE	(I) One 480hp Curtiss D-12 (Felix); (IA) Rolls-Royce FXIIA (later Kestrel IIA)
WINGSPAN	(Prototype) 33ft 6ins (Production) 37ft 8in
LENGTH	28ft 3in
HEIGHT	10ft 8in
WING AREA	(Production) 324 sq ft
TARE WEIGHT	2,609lb
LOADED WEIGHT	(I) 4,170lb; (IA) 4,640lb
MAX SPEED	(I) 156mph at sea level; (IA) 160mph at sea level
CLIMB	2,000ft in 1min 48secs
SERVICE CEILING	17,000ft
RANGE	500 miles

Production

Twenty-eight Fairey Foxes were built between 1924 and 1927 serialled Mk I, J7941–J7958, J8423–J8427; Mk IA J9025–J9028 and J9515.

J9026 was an example of a late production Fox I which was fitted with a Kestrel IIA engine to become a Mk IA. The aircraft is pictured being demonstrated by a 12 Squadron pilot in May 1929. (*Aeroplane*)

Only five Foxes were built to Mk IA standard from new, the rest were converted from the original batch of Mk Is. This is J7945, which was delivered to 12 Squadron in July 1926, converted to a Mk IA and returned to the unit in March 1929. (Via Martyn Chorlton)

Ferret I, II and III

Development
Initially designed to FAA Specification 37/22, the next aircraft to be built by Fairey was the company's first all-metal aircraft. The Ferret, which was effectively a development of the IIID and is often referred to as the missing 'IIIE', was not received with great enthusiasm by the FAA, but a second specification, 22/26, saw the aircraft being put forward as a DH.9A and F.2B replacement.

Design
The all-metal, three-seater Ferret had a fuselage covered in sheet aluminium, while the rest of airframe was covered in fabric. Although based on the IIID, the Ferret was smaller; its wingspan was 7ft shorter, and its weight was approximately 25 per cent less. The first of three prototypes was powered by a 400hp Jaguar IV engine, while the next two aircraft had a 425hp Jupiter engine. The undercarriage had an oleo V-strut, and the wings, both upper and lower, were staggered and swept-back while the tail surfaces remained in the traditional Fairey design.

Service
The first aircraft, Ferret I, serial N190, was first flown from Northolt by Norman Macmillan on 5 June 1925. Not long after, the aircraft was transferred to the Aeroplane and Armament Experimental Establishment (A&AEE) for flight trials in competition with the Hawker Hedgehog and Blackburn Airedale, both vying for a production from Specification 37/22. However, part way through the trials, 37/22 was abandoned, and Specification 26/27 was introduced, which called for a general-purpose aircraft to replace the DH.9A.

The second Ferret, N191, was already close to completion when 37/22 was withdrawn, but the third and final Ferret, N192, was at a stage where it could be redesigned to compete for 26/27. The aircraft was now a two-seater and was competing against the Bristol Beaver, de Havilland DH.9J Stag, DH.65 Hound, IIIF, Gloster Goral, Vickers Vixen VI, Vickers Valiant and the Westland Wapiti. The Ferret reached the final stages of the flight trials in May 1927, and, until problems began occurring with the engine and propeller, it was on the verge of winning the competition outright. However, the Ferret failed but Fairey still won a major production for the IIIF.

Technical data – Ferret I, II and III	
ENGINE	(I) One 400hp Armstrong Siddeley Jaguar IV 14-cylinder two-row radial; (II and III) One 425hp Bristol Jupiter nine-cylinder radial
WINGSPAN	(I) 39ft 10in; (II and III) 40ft 7in
LENGTH	29ft 6in
WING AREA	380 sq ft
EMPTY WEIGHT	(III) 2,583lb
LOADED WEIGHT	(III) 4,179lb
MAX SPEED	(III) 132mph at sea level
CLIMB	(III) 5,000ft in 6mins 30secs
SERVICE CEILING	(III) 15,000ft

A very rare image of the first Ferret Mk I, N190, during its service with the Aeroplane and Armament Experimental Establishment (A&AEE), 22 Squadron, at Martlesham Heath between August 1926 and March 1928. (Via Martyn Chorlton)

Fairey Ferret II. (Key Archive)

Firefly I

Development
It would not be unrealistic to surmise that the Fairey Firefly I was designed as an escort fighter for the Fox bomber. Both were creations of Marcel Lobelle, and both were designed around the same Curtiss D-12 engine, which was renamed Felix by Fairey. Both aircraft were made from wood, and both were private ventures, and, while only one Firefly I would be built, the Fox had orders, albeit in small numbers.

Design
The Firefly was conceived in March 1924, after Fairey gained a licence to build the D-12 engine in Britain. A request was made to the Air Ministry for its latest requirements for a single-seat fighter, from whence the reply stated seating for a single pilot, two forward-firing machine guns with room for 1,200 rounds and fuel capacity large enough for at least two hours' endurance. To back up this information, the Air Ministry also, generously, gave Fairey the specifications for the Napier Lion IV powered Gloster Gorcock and the future Rolls-Royce Condor IV powered Hawker Hornbill. Both of these latter aircraft would ultimately become nothing more than research aircraft.

Service
The sole Fairey Firefly I (c/n F.572) was flown for the first time by Norman Macmillan from Northolt on 9 November 1925. Manufacturer's trials were completed on 2 December, and, following flight testing by the A&AEE, the Air Ministry report was very positive. The view for the pilot was one particular feature of the Firefly, a very important factor for a fighter, and one that was commented on as being far superior to the visibility from a Gloster Gamecock or Armstrong Whitworth Siskin. However, the Air Ministry report ended bluntly with the statement, 'not likely to buy more than one unless redesigned with a British engine'. It was then proposed that the fighter be fitted with the 490hp Rolls-Royce F.10 (later named Kestrel) engine, which, following Air Ministry calculations, should have given the Firefly an improved maximum speed and greater ceiling.

Fairey set about redesigning the Firefly to take the geared Rolls-Royce F.II, which was much heavier and larger than the original US D-12 powerplant. As a result, on paper at least, Fairey predicted that a Rolls-Royce powered Firefly I would be a failure, and the company withdrew the offer to the Air Ministry of its latest fighter design.

Technical data – Firefly I	
ENGINE	One 430hp Curtiss D-12C twelve-cylinder vee liquid-cooled engine
WINGSPAN	31ft 6in
LENGTH	24ft 10in
HEIGHT	9ft 1in
LOADED WEIGHT	2,724lb
MAX SPEED	185mph
CLIMB	5,000ft in 2mins 24secs

The only Fairey Firefly I built was never given a military serial, only being referred to by its construction number, F.572. (Via Martyn Chorlton)

Fairey Firefly I. (Key Archive)

IIIF

Development
The last of the long line of III series aircraft, the IIIF was produced in greater numbers than any other British operational aircraft from the end of World War One to the mid-1930s (except the Hawker Hart family). A refined version of the IIID, over 600 were built.

Design
Following the failure of Specification 37/22 for a three-seat deck-landing reconnaissance aircraft to replace the Blackburn and Bison, new Specification 19/24 for a three-seat fleet reconnaissance aircraft for the FAA and a two-seat general-purpose aircraft for the RAF, was specifically written for the IIIF. In late 1926 to early 1927, two prototypes, N198 and N225, were ordered for evaluation. N198 was first flown by Norman Macmillan on 19 March 1926. Constructed with a wood and metal composite fuselage and wooden wings, the first aircraft was flown as a landplane but, not long after, was sent to Hamble, fitted with a pair of Fairey metal floats and sent for further evaluation to the MAEE at Felixstowe.

Operational service
The new IIIF was well received, and, to hasten its entry into service, the last ten IIIDs built were converted to IIIF standard and shipped to Aboukir, Egypt, for theatre trials with 5 and 60 squadrons. These trials were complete by April 1927, and the first of many production orders followed, the initial examples being IIIF Mk IV C/M (GPs). The majority went on to serve with 8 Squadron in Aden and 207 Squadron at Eastchurch.

The FAA received its aircraft in May 1927 when the IIIF Mk I entered service with 443 (Composite) Flight for active service on board HMS *Furious*. Service with Catapult Flights on board warships of the 2nd, 6th and 8th Cruiser Squadrons soon followed. By December 1927, the first Mk IVs had arrived with the RAF's first front-line unit, 47 (General Purpose) Squadron at Khartoum, while the FAA had established 440, 445, 446 (Fleet Spotter Reconnaissance) Flights on board HMS *Argus* and *Courageous*.

Technical data – IIIF MK I Landplane, MK II Seaplane, MK IIIM/BGP Landplane, MKIIIM/B Seaplane	
ENGINE	One Napier Lion VA, XI or XIA 12-cylinder broad-arrow liquid-cooled engine
WINGSPAN	45ft 9in
LENGTH	(I) 33ft 10in; (II and III Sea) 35ft 6in; (III Land) 34ft; (IV) 36ft 9in
HEIGHT	(I) 11ft 3in; (II) 12ft 7in; (III Land) 12ft 9in; (III Sea) 14ft; (IV) 14ft 2in
WING AREA	(Prototype) 443 sq ft
LOADED WEIGHT	(I) 5,120lb; (II) 5,300lb; (III Land) 5,874lb; (III Sea) 6,301lb; (IV) 6,041lb
MAX SPEED	(I) 150mph; (II) 135mph; (III Land) 136mph; (III Sea); 130mph; (IV) 120mph at 10,000ft
CLIMB	(III Land) 5,000ft in 5mins 34secs; (III Sea) 5,000ft in 6mins 25secs
SERVICE CEILING	(III Sea) 20,000ft
ENDURANCE	(III Sea) 3 to 4hrs

The majority of IIIFs supplied to the RAF were the Mk IV, although 61 Mk Is and IIIs were also transferred to the RAF over a period of time. The sub-variant of the Mk IV was designated C/M, which indicated the aircraft was of a composite metal and wood construction while others were designated as M/As, which meant an all-metal construction.

The IIIF was phased out of frontline RAF service in 1935 while the FAA continued to use the type operationally until the following year, although several examples remained on strength until 1941.

Production

Fifty-five Mk Is were built, followed by 33 Mk IIs, 291 Mk IIIs and 243 Mk IVs. The Mk V variant became the Gordon, while the Mk VI became the Seal.

Right: Originally delivered to 450 Flight at Gosport for HMS *Courageous* in October 1930, IIIF Mk IIIB, S1487 '86' is pictured during its tour of duty with 824 Squadron with HMS *Eagle*. (*Aeroplane*)

Below: S1795 was one of a batch of 68 IIIF Mk IIIBs built to Contract No.110958/31 and first delivered to the FAA Pool at Gosport in December 1931. The aircraft was then transferred to the School of Naval Co-Operation at Lee-on-Solent and coded 'H' in August 1932. (*Aeroplane*)

Firefly II

Development
Another private venture designed by Marcel Lobelle, the Firefly II had little in common with its predecessor other than being a single-seat biplane fighter. The Firefly II was already being prepared on the drawing board when Specification F.20/27 was issued, calling for a fast-climbing, single-seat interceptor fighter powered by a radial engine. The latter powerplant was soon dispensed with in favour of a liquid-cooled in-line engine, which was in keeping with Lobelle's thinking around fighter design at the time.

Design
The Mk II was structurally different from the Mk I, and the wings were prominently staggered with 'N'-shaped interplane struts, while power was provided by a 480hp F.XIS engine. The Fairey II was also modified by replacing the retractable radiator and interconnected surface-cooling system with a fixed radiator under the fuselage between the undercarriage legs. The construction of the fuselage, wings, tail, undercarriage and interplane struts was also changed, and the wires that joined the pairs of ailerons were replaced by a single strut. Fuel capacity rose to 52 gallons, split between a 40-gallon main tank and a 12-gallon gravity tank. The open cockpit was heated to such a degree that the pilot could make notes with bare hands at 21,000ft; a height where the outside air temperature would be around -34 degrees Celsius.

Operational service
First flown on 5 February 1929, the Firefly II (c/n F.1130) was entered into that year's 'interceptor' competition at the Aeroplane and Armament Experimental Establishment (A&AEE) at Martlesham Heath. Unfortunately for Fairey, the Firefly II was marginally beaten by the Hawker Hornet (developed into the Fury and ordered for RAF in 1930). Despite having superior speed, the aircraft lost out because of heavy controls and the fact that it was made of wood. Rebuilt with a metal fuselage and redesignated as the Firefly IIM, the fighter first flew in its new guise from Northolt on 6 January 1930. In June 1930, the Mk IIM was demonstrated at the RAF Display at Hendon, and it was here that it caught the attention of several potential overseas customers, including the Belgians.

Registered as G-ABCN, the Firefly IIM was flown to Belgium by Chris Staniland on 23 July 1930, where it was demonstrated against the Avia B.H.33 and the Dewoitine D.27. The Firefly won the day, and by late summer 1930, a contract was signed for an initial order of 25 aircraft. Built at Hayes but

Technical data – Firefly II and IIM	
ENGINE	One 480hp Rolls-Royce F.XIS (later named Kestrel IIS) 12-cylinder vee liquid-cooled
WINGSPAN	(II) 30ft 8in; (IIM) 31ft 6in
LENGTH	24ft 8in
HEIGHT	(II) 9ft 1in; (IIM) 9ft 4in
EMPTY WEIGHT	(Equipped) 2,387lb
LOADED WEIGHT	3,285lb
MAX SPEED	175mph at sea level
CLIMB	19,685ft in 10mins 55secs
SERVICE CEILING	30,840ft

assembled in Belgium, a follow up order for 20 more Firefly IIMs soon followed, which would be built by a new associated company called Avions Fairey, which was formed on 12 September 1931 at Gosselies, near Charleroi, Belgium.

The Firefly IIM joined the Belgian Air Force in late 1931, the first unit to receive it being 1 Squadron, 1 Group, at Schaffen. Other units followed, and up to the German invasion in May 1940, 50 Fireflies were still in service. Several were also shipped to North Africa in June 1940, and several were still parked on the airfield at Oran's La Sénia in November 1942.

Production

Eighty-eight Firefly IIMs were built; the first 25 (c/n F.1489 to F.1513) were built at Hayes, the remainder by Avions Fairey, totalling 62 (c/ns F.1651 to F.1670, F.1693 to F.1722, F.1928 to F.1933 and F.2032 to F.2037). One aircraft (F.1876) was built for sale in the Soviet Union.

Right: Labelled as the F.1130 (MOD), this is the original Firefly II following modification to Mk IIM and registered as G-ABCN. The aircraft remained in use by Fairey until 1932. (Via Martyn Chorlton)

Below: F.1130 as the Firefly IIM is pictured in June 1930, only weeks before it was successfully demonstrated displaying the serial G-ABCN. (Via Martyn Chorlton)

Firefly IIIM and IV

Development
Another private venture, also by the name of Firefly, was running alongside the Mk II and Mk IIIM during 1929. This was being designed to meet Royal Navy Specification N.21/26, which called for a single-seat carrier/deck-landing fighter for service with the FAA. Therefore, the Firefly III (c/n F.1137) was born, which, on the surface, resembled the Mk II.

Design
The Firefly III had a larger wing, with a span of 33ft 6in, exactly 2ft longer than the Mk II. Powered by a Rolls-Royce F.XIMS (moderately supercharged) engine, it was first flown in this configuration by Norman Macmillan on 17 May 1929. As with the Mk II before, however, the Firefly III was returned to the Hayes factory for a period of six months to re-emerge as the Mk IIIM on 2 December. As well as many metal parts being incorporated, the Firefly IIIM was strengthened for catapult operations, fitted with floatation gear and wheel brakes and was capable of carrying a quartet of 20lb bombs. The engine was also replaced by a fully supercharged Rolls-Royce F.XIS.

Operational service
The Firefly IIIM was first flown on 10 December 1929 by Macmillan and then delivered to Martlesham Heath on 1 March 1930 for its first batch of tests. By June, the Mk IIIM began carrier trials aboard HMS *Furious*. The Armstrong Whitworth Starling, Hawker Hornet and Vickers 177 were also trialled at the same time, but eventually, the Firefly IIIM lost out to Hawker again, when N.21/26 was won by the Hawker Norn, later renamed the Nimrod. In September 1930, the Mk IIIM displayed the registration G-ABFH but would later appear with the military serial S1592. The Mk IIIM S1592 was converted to a twin-float aircraft in early 1931 and, on 12 March, was delivered to the MAEE at Felixstowe for flight testing. During August and September 1932, S1592, along with the Fairey Fleetwing, joined the RAF's High-Speed Flight, which was preparing for that year's Schneider Trophy competition. The aircraft was employed for floatplane training and for weather checks before returning to the MAEE for additional testing.

Technical data – Firefly IIIM and IV	
ENGINE	(IIIM); One Rolls-Royce F.XIMS and later one F.XIS (fully supercharged); (IV) One 785hp Hispano-Suiza 12Xbrs 12-cylinder vee liquid-cooled and one Rolls-Royce Kestrel IIS
WINGSPAN	33ft 6in
LENGTH	25ft 4in
HEIGHT	9ft 10in
EMPTY WEIGHT	(IV) 2,468lb
LOADED WEIGHT	(IIIM) 3,816lb; (IV) 3,405lb
MAX SPEED	(IIIM) 188mph at sea level; (IV) 192mph at sea level
CLIMB	(IIIM) 5,000ft in 2mins 48secs; (IV) 13,120ft in 4mins 29secs
SERVICE CEILING	(IV) 29,520ft

By October 1931, S1592, according to MAEE records, had completed 137 flying hours, 81 one of which were on floats. By 1932, the floats had been replaced by a neatly spatted undercarriage, and, after a spell with the RAE, the sole Firefly IIIM was last recorded as joining the A&AEE in June 1934.

A pair of Belgian-built Mk IIMs were converted to Mk IV standard in 1933 by fitting a Hispano-Suiza 12-cylinder engine in one and a Rolls-Royce Kestrel IIS in the other. One aircraft, A.F.5050 (AF for Avions Fairey), was purchased back by the parent company and flight tested by Chris Staniland at Harmondsworth on 24 November 1933. After a short period of testing, it was apparent that the performance from either engine was not much better than the original Mk IIM.

The Fairey IIIM, S1592, in its final and quite possibly most pleasing form with stylish wheel spats, pictured in July 1932 whilst serving with the RAE at Farnborough. (Via Martyn Chorlton)

S1592 pictured during its service with the RAF High Speed Flight off Calshot, in preparation for the 1931 Schneider Trophy race. (Via Martyn Chorlton)

Long-range Monoplane I and II

Development
The Fairey Long-range Monoplane came about in 1927 because of the failure of the Hawker Horsley to capture the world's long-distance record for Britain. This expensive exercise was supported by the Air Ministry, and, when the cost of the project was questioned in the Commons, supporters of the idea managed to veil the aircraft as a valuable asset in exploring long-distance flight. This was partly true, and, if the aircraft was successful, it could potentially create both a great deal of publicity for the RAF and kudos for Britain.

Design
One of the most attractive aircraft of its day, the story of the Long-range Monoplane began in December 1927 when the Air Ministry issued draft Specification 33/27, which was received with great enthusiasm by Fairey's chief engineer, Major T. M. Barlow. The specification was an open one, and designs presented for the aircraft were as a biplane, as well as a high-wing and low-wing monoplane, all of which were studied. A high-wing cantilever arrangement was chosen following successful wind tunnel testing. The need for a gravity feed fuel system to the engine from large fuel tanks, with a capacity of 1,000 gallons in the wing, helped to secure a high-wing design. Power was provided by a Napier Lion XIA, and flight instruments, as well as the standard array, included a rate-of-turn indicator, which was a very rare instrument in 1928.

Operational service
The first of two Long-range Monoplanes, J9479, made its maiden flight from Northolt on 14 November 1928 in the hands of Squadron Leader A. G. Jones-Williams and Flight Lieutenant F. V. Major. After preliminary testing, the aircraft was flown to Cranwell, where a specially tuned Lion XIA was fitted in preparation for the aircraft's record breaking flight in the spring of 1929. The task of fitting the new engine did not go smoothly, and it was not until 8 December that J9479 was returned to Northolt for further flight testing and this resulted in further engine changes. A 24-hour endurance flight, which was initially planned to take place in December 1928, was actually carried out on 22/23 March 1929. During this flight, it was calculated that J9479 could potentially fly 5,200 to 5,500 miles, despite a valve in the engine burning out.

By this time, the original idea of carrying out the first flight to South Africa was postponed, but an alternative trip to India was feasible. On 24 April 1929, Squadron Leader Jones-Williams and

Technical data – Long-Range Monoplane I and II	
ENGINE	One 570hp Napier Lion XIA
WINGSPAN	82ft
LENGTH	48ft 6in
HEIGHT	12ft
WING AREA	900 sq ft
LOADED WEIGHT	(I) 16,000lb; (II) 17,500lb
ESIMATED STILL-AIR RANGE	(I) 4,900 miles; (II) 5,550 miles
ACTUAL TAKE-OFF DISTANCE	(I) 3,705ft; (II) 4,500ft

Flight Lieutenant N. H. Jenkins took off from Cranwell at 0957hrs and, 50hrs 37mins later, landed at Karachi on 26 April. The intended destination was Bangalore, which would have broken the distance record, but unexpectedly strong headwinds forced J9479 down early, with just eight gallons of fuel remaining. The original South African flight was attempted on 16 December 1929, when, once again, Jones-Williams and Jenkins departed Cranwell. Sadly, the aircraft hit high ground south of Tunis, killing both crew and destroying J9479.

In 1931, a second Long-range Monoplane was built, K1991, constructed to Air Ministry Specification 14/30. K1991 only differed from the original aircraft in having an automatic pilot, revised fuel system and spatted wheels. On 27/28 October, in the hands of Squadron Leader O. R. Gayford and Flight Lieutenant D. L. G. Bett, K1991 was flown from Cranwell to Abu Sueir, Egypt, in 31½ hours; a distance of 2,857 miles.

It was not until February 1933 that the hard work of Fairey and the RAF bore fruit. On 6 February, Squadron Leader Gayford and Flight Lieutenant G. E. Nicholetts left Cranwell at 0710hrs and landed at Walvis Bay, southwest Africa, at 1635hrs on 8 February. The distance of 5,309 miles in 57hrs 25mins captured the world's long-distance record for Britain.

Squadron Leader A. G. Jones-Williams and Flight Lieutenant N. H. Jenkins are pictured in front of J9479 at Karachi in April 1929; the distance covered was 4,130 miles in 50hrs 37mins. (Via Martyn Chorlton)

The second Long-range Monoplane, K1991, prior to its maiden flight on 30 June 1931. K1991 differed from its predecessor in several subtle ways, including a different fuel system, landing-wheel spats, and an automatic pilot by the name of 'George', a nickname that the device was stuck with for many years after. (Via Martyn Chorlton)

Fleetwing

Development
The FAA had desired a new twin-seat spotter reconnaissance aircraft from 1926. The same year, Specification O.22/26 was issued for such a machine. Marcel Lobelle responded in typical style by designing a very clean aircraft, not dissimilar in appearance to the attractive Fox.

Design
The Fleetwing followed the same construction technique as the Fox IIM, with an all-metal, steel tube fuselage and steel-strip wing spars. Power was initially provided by a Kestrel I and later by a moderately supercharged Kestrel IIMS. The Fleetwing first flew with wooden wings, but, following trials with the A&AEE, these were replaced by metal ones, the fin area was increased and a horn balance was fitted to the rudder.

Armament was a single Vickers machine gun, which was fired through a blast trough located on the port side of the engine cowling by the pilot, while the observer/gunner was equipped with a Lewis machine gun mounted on a Fairey high-speed mounting. Four 20lb bombs could be carried on racks under the port wing. Specification O.22/26 was a hotly contested requirement, and Blackburn, Short Brothers and Hawker also competed. The all-dominant Hawker won the day yet again, this time with a modified version of the Hart, which would emerge as the Osprey. However, the Fleetwing achieved a commendable second place during the evaluation period, which was carried out at the MAEE during May and June 1930.

Operational service
The one and only Fleetwing (c/n F.1132) was serialled N235 and flew for the first time in the hands of Norman Macmillan on 16 May 1929 from Northolt. Following preliminary trials at Martlesham Heath, the aircraft performed deck trials on board HMS *Furious* in June. Following a return to Fairey for the early modifications, the Fleetwing was back in the air by September and, in October 1929, carried out final service trials at Martlesham. As well as the O.22/26 trials, the Fleetwing also operated alongside the prototype Hart and Blackburn Nautilus as part of 405 Flight on HMS *Furious* from January to March 1930. Later, in April 1932, the Fleetwing also served aboard HMS *Norfolk* for various trials, including extensive catapult work. Twenty-nine flights were carried out from *Norfolk*, the final one on 18 July, which ended in a forced landing in heavy seas alongside the ship. Unfortunately, the float undercarriage collapsed and sufficient additional damage was caused during the recovery to warrant the Fleetwing being written off. N235 had proved to be a very useful aircraft during its three-year career its duties included being used as hack, along with the Firefly III, as part of the RAF High Speed Flight, during its build up to the Schneider Trophy race in 1931.

Fleetwing

Technical data – Fleetwing Landplane and Floatplane	
ENGINE	One Rolls-Royce F.XI (Kestrel I) and later a Rolls-Royce Kestrel IIMS
WINGSPAN	37ft
LENGTH	(Land) 29ft 4in; (Sea) 32ft
HEIGHT	(Land) 11ft 5in; (Sea) 12ft 6in
WING AREA	363 sq ft
LOADED WEIGHT	(Land) 4,737lb; (Sea) 5,100lb
MAX SPEED	(Land) 169mph; (Sea) 156mph
CLIMB RATE	(Land) 5,000ft in 4mins 12secs; (Sea) 5,000ft in 5mins 48secs

Above: The only Fairey Fleetwing was N235, which is shown here in its original form in May 1929 with wire-connected ailerons and standard rudder without a horn-balance. (*Aeroplane*)

Right: N235 is seen here taxiing out for training for the 1931 Schneider Trophy race. (Key Archive)

Fox II, III, IV and V

Development
The Fox II came about in haste after Fairey failed to be invited to tender for Specification 12/26 for a two-seat high-performance day bomber, despite the fact that the Fox I was already in RAF service. The Fox IIM, an all-metal successor of the Fox I and Mk IA, failed to win the specification, which was won by the Hawker Hart, but, along with the Firefly proved to be a success in Belgium, where the aircraft and its many derivatives were built in healthy numbers.

Design
Designed by Marcel Lobelle and P. A. Ralli, the structure, aerodynamics and arrangement were very different from the Fox I. Built from steel with a tubular structured fuselage, the aircraft was fabric-covered, and the main wing spars were made of drawn high-tensile strip. The Fox II also introduced a horn-balanced rudder and fin, which would continue to be used on the Seal, Gordon II and several other Fairey biplanes. Armament was the same as the Fox I, while power, for the prototype at least, was provided by 480hp supercharged F.XIB (later Kestrel IB).

Operational service
The prototype, designated as the Fox IIM and serialled J9834, first took to the air from Northolt on 25 October 1929, flown by Norman Macmillan. Later registered as G-ABFG, the prototype was flown to Belgium in late 1930 by Chris Staniland for a demonstration. Subsequent negotiations were successful, on the condition that the type was maintained, repaired and later assembled in Belgium.

A contract was signed for a dozen Hayes-built Foxes, the first of which flew in December 1931 and was delivered to the Belgian Air Force a few weeks later. Simply designated the Fox II, these were powered by a supercharged Kestrel IIS engine, and, following the establishment of Avions Fairey, a further 31 were built under licence, including a pair of Fox IISs that were dual-controlled.

The Fox III (F.1842) was a Hayes-built demonstrator that first flew on 22 June 1933, appearing at the SBAC display at Hendon just four days later. Registered as G-ABBY, the aircraft was modified into a reconnaissance fighter with a pair of forward-firing machine-guns and spatted undercarriage. It was later heavily demonstrated in the Far East but failed to secure any orders. The follow-up Mk IIIs were built in Belgium in three variants, the first powered by a Kestrel IIS with twin forward-firing machine-guns. The second variant was a trainer, designated as Fox IIIS with a Kestrel IIMS, and finally the most prolific mark was the Fox IIIC, the 'C' being for combat. Approximately 48 IIICs are believed to have been built with twin machine-guns and an enclosed cockpit. The later production IIICs were powered by a 600hp Kestrel V engine, and these were designated as the Fox V.

Technical data – Fox II, III, IV and V	
ENGINE	(IIM) One 480hp Rolls-Royce F.XIB (later Kestrel IB); (II) One 480hp Kestrel IIS; (III) One 525hp Kestrel IIMS; (Trainer) One 360hp Armstrong Siddeley Serval
WINGSPAN	38ft
LENGTH	29ft 10in
HEIGHT	10ft
LOADED WEIGHT	4,665lb
MAX SPEED	189mph
CEILING	28,860ft

Pictured at the Great West aerodrome, three Hayes-built Fairey Fox IIs await delivery by Belgian pilots, Captain Guillaume, Adjt Caryn and Verboomen in January 1932. (*Aeroplane*)

Hendon/Night Bomber

Development
The Hendon broke the company mould in more ways than one, being Fairey's only deviation towards a heavy bomber design and the first twin-engined aircraft since the F.2 of 1917. Originally named the Fairey Night Bomber (the name Hendon was not attached until October 1934), the aircraft was designed to the 1927 Specification B/19/27. This specification, of which all other entrants were biplanes, was eventually won by the stately Handley Page Heyford, leaving the advanced design of Hendon adrift.

Design
Designed by D. L. Hollis Williams and P. A. Rallis, who had produced the unique Long-range Monoplane, the Hendon was heavily influenced by the duo's knowledge of stressing and aerodynamics. The all-metal, low- and deep-wing cantilever 'Fairey Night-bomber', as it was first penned in 1927, had a host of novel features including an internal bomb bay, which could accommodate the latest 1,000lb bombs, and a fully streamlined undercarriage. There was an internal corrugated walkway, which traversed from the nose to the tail gunner's position. This was made possible by offsetting the pilot's cockpit, which, unusually for the day, was fitted with a canopy.

Operational service
The prototype, K1695, having been built at Hayes, was transported to the aerodrome at Harmondsworth (aka Great West, and later Heathrow) where it was reassembled in November 1930. On 17 November, Fairey's chief test pilot, Norman Macmillan, carried out taxiing trials, and, eight days later, with the chief designer, Hollis Williams, on board, the Hendon made its maiden flight.

On 15 March 1931, K1695 overran the airfield boundary and was temporarily returned to the workshops, from where it re-emerged with a pair of Rolls-Royce Kestrel II engines, rather than the original Bristol Jupiter Xs.

Technical data – Hendon	
ENGINE	(Prototype) Two 525hp Bristol Jupiter XFs; (II) Two 695hp Rolls-Royce Kestrel VIs fully supercharged
WINGSPAN	101ft 9in
LENGTH	60ft 9in
HEIGHT	18ft 9in
WING AREA	1,447 sq ft
EMPTY WEIGHT	12,773lb
LOADED WEIGHT	20,000lb
MAX SPEED	155mph at 15,000ft
CRUISING SPEED	133 mph at 15,000ft
RATE OF CLIMB	940 ft/min
CLIMB	10,000ft in 15mins
SERVICE CEILING	21,400ft
RANGE	1,360 miles

Considering the Hendon was designed to a 1927 Specification, the Air Ministry still ordered 14 examples as a stop gap prior to the arrival of the Vickers Wellington and the Armstrong Whitworth Whitley. The first production aircraft flew from Barton on 24 September 1936 and entered service with 38 Squadron at Mildenhall in November. The production aircraft were designated as Hendon IIs, as they were fitted with Kestrel VI engines with more power, and an enclosed turret was provided for the front gunner rather than an open cockpit. Fairey three-blade propellers were also fitted in place of the Hendon Is wooden two-blade types. The Hendon II also served with 115 Squadron when 'B' Flight of 38 Squadron was used to reform the new unit at Marham on 15 June 1937. By August, 115 Squadron had re-equipped with the Harrow, while 38 Squadron continued to operate the Hendon II until January 1939, when it was replaced by the Wellington.

Production

Fifteen Hendons were built, including one prototype, K1695, plus K5085–K5098. A further order for 62 Hendons was later cancelled.

Above: With Flight Lieutenant Chris S. Staniland at the controls, the prototype Fairey Hendon, K1695, takes off from Harmondsworth aerodrome, which is better known today as Heathrow. (Via Martyn Chorlton)

Right: The prototype Hendon at the A&AEE, Martlesham Heath, in May 1925, complete with canopy, enclosed front turret (mock-up in this view) and a pair of Kestrel VI engines. (Via Martyn Chorlton)

Gordon I and II

Development
With the arrival of the more powerful and lighter Panther IIA engine, the opportunity arose to re-engine the IIIF. However, rather than continue the series by making the latest Fairey design, the IIIF Mk V, it was deemed that there were sufficient changes from its predecessors to give the aircraft a separate name – Gordon.

Design
Fairey's own proposal to re-engine the IIIF resulted in Specification 18/30, which was simply described as 'an IIIF replacement', the Panther-engined Gordon being the only entrant. The new engine saw a marked improvement in performance, thanks to the radial being lighter and more fuel-efficient, the latter resulted in a 10 per cent improvement in air mileage per gallon. The distance covered during take-off was reduced by 15 per cent, and the service ceiling rose by a further 10 per cent.

The chosen airframe was IIIF Mk IV M/A K1697, which, while still on the production line, was re-engined and given a general tidy up. Designated as the prototype Gordon, K1697 first took to the air from Harmondsworth on 3 March 1931 in the hands of Chris Staniland.

Operational service
By the end of March, performance tests had already been carried out by the A&AEE, and, in no time at all, an initial order of 28 Gordons, originally scheduled to be built as IIIF Mk IVBs, was placed. The first 12 off the line were built as bombers, complete with a prone bomb aimer's position for service with 40 Squadron at Upper Heyford, from April 1931. The remaining 14 Gordons were shipped to the Middle East to serve with 6 Squadron at Ramleh.

A bigger order for 47 Gordons followed, allowing 35 Squadron at Bircham Newton to retire its IIIFs from July 1932. 14 Squadron at Ramleh followed in July 1932, and 4 FTS began receiving dual-control versions by the end of the year as well. The biggest and final order for 87 Gordons saw the type being delivered to the RAF between May 1932 and January 1933. An improved version, the

Technical data – Gordon I	
ENGINE	One 525hp Armstrong Siddeley Panther IIA 14-cylinder two-row radial
WINGSPAN	45ft 9in
LENGTH	36ft 9in
HEIGHT	14ft 2in
WING AREA	438 sq ft
EMPTY WEIGHT	3,500lb
LOADED WEIGHT	5,906lb
MAX SPEED	145mph at 3,000ft
CRUISING SPEED	110mph
INITIAL CLIMB	1,000ft/min
SERVICE CEILING	22,000ft
RANGE	600 miles

Gordon II, began arriving in the Middle East in 1934. The Mk II had a new fin and rudder with horn balance, a modified rear fuselage and Frise ailerons. The Royal New Zealand Air Force would later receive 13 Mk IIs and a few Mk Is. By September 1939, the Gordon was withdrawn from operational service, but at least 40 examples remained on RAF strength, all serving in a secondary role until the middle of 1941.

Production

There were 162 Gordon Is built in the serial ranges: K1721–K1748, K2603–K2649 and K2683–K2769. Twenty-four Gordon IIs were built, K3986–K4009, and 79 IIIFs were also converted in the serial ranges J9062–J9828, K1159–K1778 and S1178–S1203.

Right: An impressive nine-ship formation of 6 Squadron's Fairey Gordons, operating out of Ismailia. (*Aeroplane*)

Below: Twenty Gordons were sold to the Brazilian government, and all but five of them were landplanes, making this photo of 1-EB-4 a rare catch. (Via Martyn Chorlton)

Seal (IIIF Mk IV)

Development
Originally designated as the IIIF MK IV, the Seal was effectively the three-seat predecessor of the Gordon II. The Seal came about because of Specification 12/29, which covered the IIIF Mk VI prior to the Mk V, which, in turn became the Gordon.

Design
The prototype, S1325, a converted IIIF, did not take to the air until 27 November 1931. At this time, the Gordon I was already on the production line, and further work was required before the Seal actually met 12/29. Once this was achieved, the Seal entered production in front of the Gordon II, and it was a production Seal, K3577, which was later converted to become the prototype Mk II.

By early 1932, the first production order for 11 Seals was placed, the type featuring Frise ailerons, a fin with a bigger aspect ratio, an 'A' frame arrester hook below the rear fuselage and a tail wheel in place of the long-serving skid.

Operational service
By the end of November 1932, the first four production aircraft were ready for delivery to 444 (Fleet Reconnaissance Catapult) and, by the end of the year, all were on board ships of the 2nd Battle Squadron in home seas. 821 Squadron was the first operational unit to receive the Seal at Gosport in April 1933. The unit embarked on HMS *Courageous* the following month for a two-year tour of duty in home waters. However, by August 1935, the carrier was serving with the Mediterranean fleet during the Abyssinian crisis.

In 1934, a second Seal unit, 820 Squadron, embarked on *Courageous* for a six-month tour of duty that saw the Seal replaced by the Blackburn Shark torpedo bomber by the end. The Fairey Seal went on to serve with eight FAA squadrons, although only four ever served at one time. Only 824 Squadron saw service east of the Suez, when HMS *Hermes* arrived in Hong Kong in January 1935. The ship served as part of the China station for the next three years, but the Seal did not; its replacement, the Swordfish, took over in April 1937, while *Hermes* was visiting Seletar in Singapore.

Technical data – Seal Landplane and Seaplane	
ENGINE	One 525hp Armstrong Siddeley Panther IIA 14-cylinder two-row radial
WINGSPAN	45ft 9in
LENGTH	(Land) 36ft 9in; (Sea) 35ft 4in
HEIGHT	(Land) 12ft 9in; (Sea) 14ft 4in
WING AREA	443.5 sq ft
LOADED WEIGHT	(Land) 6,000lb; (Sea) 6,400lb
MAX SPEED	(Land) 138mph; (Sea) 129mph
CLIMB	5,000ft in 5.35mins
SERVICE CEILING	(Land) 17,000ft; (Sea) 13,900ft
ENDURANCE	4 to 5hrs

Production

Ninety-one Seals were built for the FAA in the serial ranges K3477–K3487, K3514–K3545, K3575–K3579, K4201–K4225 and K4779–K4796. Six Seals were sold to Peru, four to Latvia, two to Chile and one to Argentina.

The first production Fairey Seal, K3477, pictured at A&AEE, Martlesham Heath, on 26 April 1933. The aircraft went on to limited service, and with only 36 flying hours to its credit, was struck off charge in February 1936. (Via Martyn Chorlton)

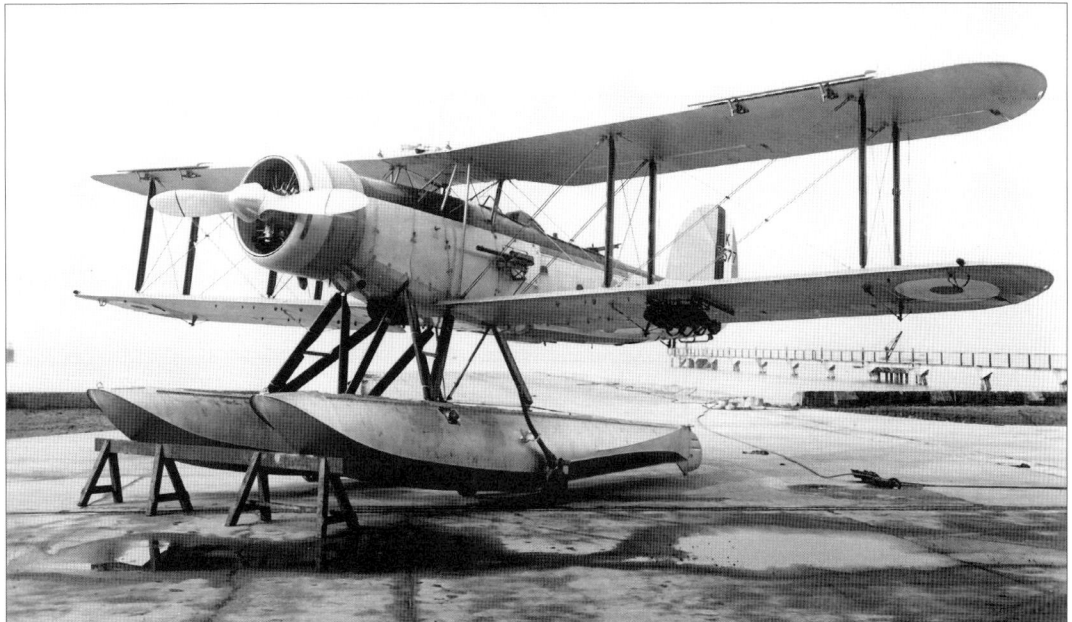

Seal K3577 pictured at MAEE, Felixstowe, for trials in early 1934. The aircraft was also experimentally fitted with a Panther VI engine in a long-chord cowling and was later converted to a landplane configuration to become the prototype Gordon II. (Via Martyn Chorlton)

Fox VI

Development
Basically a re-engined Fox IIIC, the Fox VI was created as a two-seat reconnaissance fighter, which was destined to be licence-built in Belgium.

Design
The story of the Fox VI began as an experiment when a Fox II (F.1753, AF.6031) was fitted with a 650hp Hispano-Suiza 12 Ybrs engine. The aircraft was first flown by Chris Staniland from Gosselies on 31 January 1934, and flight testing continued in Britain while the Fox VI was loaned to Fairey.
The aircraft had a fully enclosed canopy, which covered both cockpits, and a spatted undercarriage, which, combined with the power of the Hispano-Suiza, helped the Fox VI to achieve a maximum speed of 227mph.

Once the Fox VI returned to Gosseilies, the engine was replaced by an 860hp 12 Ydrs engine, and its wheel spats were removed. By now, the experimental aircraft had turned into an official prototype. In August 1934, the aircraft was demonstrated by S. H. G. Trower in front of a Belgian military mission at Gosselies, and, not long after, was ordered into production.

Operational service
The Fox VI served the Belgian Air Force in two variants, the Mk VIC and the Mk VIR, the final letter relating to combat and reconnaissance, respectively. On top of these two duties, the Fox VI was also employed as a day and night fighter and trainer, at least four aircraft being converted with dual controls. The Fox VI served with the following Belgian units from 1935 to 1940; 7/IV/1 'Méphisto' at Goetsenhoven and Lonzee, 5/III/2 'Aigle Bleu' and 6/III/2 'Aigle Rouge' at Nivelles and Vissenaken. The only other operator of the Fox VI was the Swiss government, which purchased F.2246 and F.2247 for evaluation. They were subsequently given the military serial numbers 871 and 872, and finally the civil registrations of HB-HAF and HB-HAK.

Production
Approximately 85 Fox VIs were built by Avions Fairey in the following serial ranges; F.2039 to F.2092; F.2232 to F.2241; F.2242 to F.2245, all dual-controlled; F.2246 and F.2247 to Switzerland and F.2238 to F.2263.

Technical data – Fox VI	
ENGINE	(Prototype) One 650hp Hispano-Suiza 12 Ybrs; (Production) One 860hp 12 Ydrs
WINGSPAN	38ft
LENGTH	30ft 1in
HEIGHT	11ft
LOADED WEIGHT	4,950lb
MAX SPEED	227mph
CLIMB	16,400ft in 6mins 30secs

The prototype Fairey Fox IV complete with canopy, twin cockpits, wheel spats and plenty of power from its Hispano-Suiza engine. This photograph was taken in September 1934. (*Aeroplane*)

G.4/31

Development
When Specification G.4/31 was first issued in July 1931, virtually the entire British aircraft industry began work to design a new general-purpose/torpedo bomber for the RAF. The specification was aimed at a replacement for the Gordon and the Westland Wapiti, but the document's requirements even outweighed what these two capable aircraft had been achieving. The new aircraft had to be capable of bombing day or night, dive-bombing by day, army co-operation, aerial photography, general reconnaissance, and casualty evacuation, not to mention the ability to operate from makeshift airfields in tropical conditions. It was clearly a tall order, but this did not stop Blackburn, Bristol, Handley Page, Hawker, Parnall, Vickers, Westland and, of course, Fairey, submitting designs and proposals for G.4/31.

Design
The Fairey G.4/31, just like the majority of others bidding for the specification, was not an attractive aircraft. When it was first rolled out, the Pegasus II.M3 engine was without a cowl, the tail surfaces were non-traditionally angular, and a pair of unsightly longitudinal strakes was attached to the rear fuselage in response to the loss of the TSR.I during a flat spin. The G.4/31 had a portly appearance, allowing for a spacious cabin inside the forward fuselage. This was accessed via the rear cockpit or a large door on the starboard side. The pilot's cockpit was offset to port, and each of the main planes had large cut-outs in their trailing edges, giving a good field of vision. Depending on the role the aircraft was carrying out, a second crew member could take up a prone position inside the cabin for bomb aiming.

Operational service
The Fairey G.4/31 was first flown by Chris Staniland on 29 March 1934. It was immediately apparent that the 635hp Pegasus engines were not delivering enough power to achieve the performance figures set out in the specification, and, with a heavy heart, it was replaced by a 750hp Armstrong Siddeley Tiger IV. The heavier Tiger was still being developed, and it was widely known that the engine was far from reliable.

Whilst the G.4/31 was re-engined, Fairey also took the opportunity to clean the aircraft up. The work including fitting wheel spats, redesigning the tail surfaces into a more rounded shape, the dispensing of a ventral fin, cowl around the engine and a Fairey metal propeller in place of the original wooden one. These modifications certainly made the aircraft more purposeful looking, and the facelift saw the aircraft being unofficially referred to as the G.4/31 Mk II.

The Mk II carried out its first flight, once again with Staniland at the controls, on 22 June 1934. Almost immediately, the Tiger engine began to play up, and virtually every flight had to be brought to a premature conclusion because of overheating problems. Regardless, the Air Ministry was informed about the engine problems before the aircraft was serialled as K3905 and delivered to the A&AEE in January 1935. Sadly for Fairey, the engine let the aircraft down, and not a single performance test was achieved. By February, K3905 was returned and later withdrawn from the battle to win Specification G.4/31.

Technical data – G.4/31	
ENGINE	One 635hp Bristol Pegasus II.M3 nine-cylinder air-cooled radial and, later, one 750hp Armstrong Siddeley Tiger IV 14-cylinder two-row radial
WINGSPAN	53ft
LENGTH	40ft 10in
HEIGHT	15ft 8ins
WING AREA	658 sq ft
EMPTY WEIGHT	6,987lb
LOADED WEIGHT	8,790lb
MAX SPEED	(bomber) 157mph at 6,500ft; (torpedo-bomber) 144mph at 6,500ft
CLIMB	(bomber) 5,000ft in 7mins 12secs
SERVICE CEILING	(bomber) 23,200ft

The Fairey G.4/31, in its original form, prior to its maiden flight on 29 March 1934. Note the un-cowled Pegasus engine and angular tail surfaces, both of which were changed before the aircraft reached Martlesham Heath. (Via Martyn Chorlton)

S.9/30 and TSR.I

Development
It seems remarkable to think that an aircraft that was designed to one specification, led to another that was designed two specifications later, both machines making their maiden flights a mere eight weeks apart. However, that is what occurred with the S.9/30, which, in turn, evolved into the TSR.I and then the TSR.II, the latter also becoming known as the Swordfish.

What actually occurred was that the Fairey designers were looking way beyond the original Specification S.9/30, which was issued in June 1930. By the time the aircraft flew in 1934, the requirement had predictably passed in favour of S.15/33, but Fairey had already been working on its TSR.I, which was intended for service with the Greek Navy. The TSR.I was then put forward as a contender for S.15/33, but despite being destroyed in a crash, the design was carried on with the TSR.II and the FAA went on to receive its greatest ever torpedo-bomber.

Design
The Fairey S.9/30, on the surface, was a two-bay biplane but was actually a single; the inboard inter-plane struts were only there to provide rigidity for when the wings were folded. A de-rated Kestrel IIMS engine powered the S.9/30, an engine that used evaporative cooling via surface-type steam condensers attached to the lower side of the upper wing. The fuselage was made of stainless-steel strip and the tube and was constructed in four sections.

The TSR.I was a privately financed project powered by a 625hp Panther radial engine and, despite being designed specifically for the Greek Navy, no orders were forthcoming. Prior to its bland designation name, the aircraft was referred to within the company walls as the 'Greek Machine'. Once the order fell through, the aircraft was re-engined with a 635hp Pegasus IIM engine cowled off with a Townend ring. The fixed undercarriage was trialled with and without spats, the rear fuselage was strengthened for deck operations and an arrester hook was fitted.

Operational service
The Fairey S.9/30 was first flown from Harmondsworth by Chris Staniland on 22 February 1934. Following its initial visit to the A&AEE, which was academic as the specification criteria had already been passed, the aircraft, serially S1706, was converted into a seaplane. Fitted with a large

Technical data – S.9/30 Land and Floatplane and TSR.I	
ENGINE	(S.9/30) One 525hp Rolls-Royce Kestrel IIMS; (TSR.I) One 625hp Armstrong Siddeley Panther VI and, later, one 635hp Bristol Pegasus IIM
WINGSPAN	(S.9/30 Land) 46ft; (folded) 17ft 10in
LENGTH	(Land) 34ft 1in; (Float) 39ft 3in
HEIGHT	(Land) 14ft; (Float) 16ft 6in
WING AREA	442 sq ft
LOADED WEIGHT	(Land) 5,740lb; (Float) 6,500lb
MAX SPEED	(Land) 147mph at 2,000ft; (Float) 136mph at 2,000ft
CLIMB	(Land) 5,000ft in 5mins 30secs; (Float) 5,000ft in 6.3mins

central float and smaller floats mounted on struts under the outer wings, S1706 was trialled at the MAEE, Felixstowe, alongside the Hawker Osprey. The S.9/30 performed well, but the derivate of the all-conquering Hart family won the day, and the Osprey was chosen instead. S1706 was struck off charge on 30 November 1936 and ended its days being used for crash barrier trials.

The TSR.1, which remained un-serialled, was first flown by Staniland on 21 March 1933 in its original Greek Navy form. Accepted as a contender for Specification S.15/33, trials were progressing well until 11 September 1933, when Staniland failed to recover from a flat spin and was forced to abandon the aircraft after 12 rotations. However, flight reports showed that the aircraft was more than capable to meet the specification, and all the knowledge and experienced gained was ploughed into the TSR.II.

The Marcel Lobelle-designed S.9/30 was first flown as a landplane with a divided undercarriage and low-pressure tyres. (Via Martyn Chorlton)

The privately funded TSR.I was fitted with a Bristol Pegasus engine inside a Townend ring, driving a Watts propeller, wheel spats and an arrester hook. (Via Martyn Chorlton)

TSR.II and Swordfish I

Development
As mentioned earlier, the roots of the TSR.II, which would be renamed the Swordfish, are firmly planted in the story of the S.9/30 and the TSR.I. Following the loss of the latter in September 1933, Marcel Lobelle immediately set to work redesigning the TSR.I to a new more advanced specification.

Design
Air Ministry Specification S.15/33 was for a Naval carrier-borne torpedo/spotter/reconnaissance (TSR) aircraft, which was a more advanced version of S.9/30. On the surface, the second aircraft, the TSR.II, was very similar to the TSR.I, only differing in having an extra bay in the fuselage and spin recovery strakes ahead of the tailplane (a lesson learned from the loss of the TSR.I).

The upper wing had a sweepback of 4 degrees to compensate for the longer fuselage, while other differences included a greater chord fin and rudder. Construction was generally similar to the TSR.I, the TSR.II having a pair of built-up steel-strip spars, duralumin ribs in the wings, steel drag struts and a steel-tube fuselage. Power was provided by a Pegasus IIM3 engine, cowled by a substantial Townend ring, driving a two-blade wooden Watts propeller, although later, a three-blade metal type became standard.

The TSR.II, serialled K4190, was first flown on 17 April 1934 by Chris Staniland and, two months later, was being trialled at Martlesham Heath, followed by the RAE, for catapult trials, then on board HMS *Courageous* for deck-landing tests.

By April 1935, the TSR.II had been renamed the Swordfish, and a pre-production order for three aircraft came, followed by a production batch of 86 aircraft. The first pre-production aircraft, K5660, was first flown on 31 December 1935.

Operational service
The Swordfish entered service in July 1936 when it joined 825 Squadron on board HMS *Glorious*, the unit having previously operated the IIIF. By the end of the year, three more FAA squadrons had re-equipped with the Swordfish, and by late 1938, three more had re-equipped, the majority of them having replaced Blackburn Sharks and Fairey Seals. This left the Swordfish as the FAA's only torpedo-bomber until the arrival of the Fairey Albacore in March 1940.

Technical data – TSR.II and Swordfish 1	
ENGINE	One 690hp Bristol Pegasus IIIM3 nine-cylinder radial
WINGSPAN	(TSR) 45ft 5in; (I) 45ft 6in
LENGTH	(TSR) 36ft 6in; (I) 35ft 8in
HEIGHT	(I) 12ft 4in
WING AREA	(TSR) 542 sq ft; (I) 607 sq ft
EMPTY WEIGHT	(I) 4,195lb
LOADED WEIGHT	(I) 7,720lb
MAX SPEED	(I) 154mph
CRUISING SPEED	(I) 131mph
SERVICE CEILING	(I) 19,250ft
DURATION	5.7hrs

By the beginning of World War Two, 13 operational FAA squadrons were equipped with the Swordfish, and a further 12 would be formed during it. On top of these, 25 operational squadrons and a further 22 second-line squadrons also operated the Swordfish and 11 catapult flights. The Swordfish I served with great distinction in all theatres of the war, but special mention should be made regarding the aircraft's involvement in the successful attack against Italian warships in Taranto harbour on 11 November 1940, and in the demise of the *Bismarck* in May 1941.

The Swordfish I also served with RAF units, 8 and 202 squadrons, between August and December 1940 and October 1940 and June 1941, respectively, with the latter operating the seaplane variant. The Swordfish outlived its operational replacement, the Albacore, by many years, mainly because of the larger aircraft's unsuitability to operate from escort carriers. It was while carrying out these duties aboard MAC ships that the Swordfish carried out its last operational duty on 21 May 1945 with 836 Squadron.

Production

In total, 992 Swordfish Mk Is were built, 692 (201 of this number were delivered in 1937 alone) of them by Fairey at Hayes and 300 of them by Blackburn at Sherburn-in-Elmet.

Right: The prototype TSR (Torpedo/Spotter/Reconnaissance) Mk II (later Swordfish), K4190, first flew on 17 April 1934. After a host of trials, the aircraft settled with A Flight/Station Flight at Gosport but, on 23 June 1938, the Swordfish overturned on landing because the brakes had been left on after a catapult take-off. The aircraft was struck off charge eight weeks later. (*Aeroplane*)

Below: K8440 takes the cable aboard HMS *Courageous* in early 1939. The Swordfish I first joined 811 Squadron on HMS *Furious* in March 1937, before joining 811 Squadron. It was coded '609', as depicted here. (*Aeroplane*)

Fantôme/Féroce

Development
The Fantôme, the Belgian-built version of which was known as the Féroce, came about because of a Belgian government requirement for a new fighter to take over from the Firefly II. The criteria for this new aircraft were tough; a maximum speed of no less than 248mph at 16,404ft, a duration of two hours at 80 per cent power, a climb rate to 16,404ft in less than six minutes and a landing speed of 75mph. It was a tough call, but again Marcel Lobelle had produced an aircraft that was more than capable.

Design
The Fantôme was an all-metal, single-bay biplane fighter with unequal-span staggered wings, which were fabric covered. The undercarriage was semi-cantilever with spatted wheels, and the ailerons were only fitted to the upper wing. Armament was a 20mm Oerlikon cannon, which could fire through the propeller hub. A pair of Browning machine guns could also be fitted in the forward upper fuselage or wings if the 20mm cannon was not installed.

Operational service
The Fantôme, coded 'F-6', was first flown from the Great West aerodrome by Chris Staniland on 6 June 1935. Registered as G-ADIF, the aircraft was demonstrated at both the RAF and the SBAC display, but while it was taking part in the competition at Evère for a new Belgian fighter, the aircraft inexplicably crashed in the landing circuit, taking the life of test pilot S. H. G. Trower. Spare parts and various assemblies were despatched to Belgium by Fairey, which was planning on building three extra aircraft. By the time the fighter, renamed Féroce, left the Avions Fairey factory at Gosselies, the Belgians had changed their fighter requirements. In the meantime though, the Soviets expressed an interest, and, after a demonstration by Staniland at Gosselies in November 1936, two were shipped, via Antwerp, to the Soviet Union.

A fourth aircraft was ordered by the Air Ministry on 11 May 1937 and, serialled L7045, was flown for the first time by F. H. Dixon from Gosselies on 4 November 1937, before being ferried back to Britain six days later. During December 1937 and January 1938, L7045 was flown from the Great West aerodrome to Farnborough, where the main point of interest was the fighter's novel armament. All of the guns were remotely controlled, loading and cocking were performed pneumatically, and compressed air was used for the trigger motors on the fuselage guns and the wing guns.

Production
Four aircraft were built, the first, G-ADIF (F.2118), was built at Hayes; F.2264 and F.2265 were sold to the Soviet Union but were later sold to Spain to serve in the Republican Air Force, where at least one of them was shot down. L7045 (F.3451) was built and delivered to Contract No.613518/37, and, following trials with the A&AEE and RAE, the aircraft was transferred to the Air Gunnery School (AGS) Rollestone on 12 December 1940 and was not struck off charge until 19 March 1943.

Technical data – Fantôme/Féroce	
ENGINE	One 925hp Hispano-Suiza 12Yers 12-cylinder vee liquid-cooled
WINGSPAN	34ft 6in
LENGTH	27ft 7in
HEIGHT	11ft 4in
WING AREA	293 sq ft
EMPTY WEIGHT	2,500lb
LOADED WEIGHT	4,120lbs
MAX SPEED	224mph at sea level; 270mph at 13,120ft
LANDING SPEED	60mph
CLIMB	13,120ft in 5mins 40secs
CEILING	36,080ft
DURATION	2hrs at a cruising speed of 217mph

Probably the cleanest and most handsome biplane fighter ever built, by 1935 the type had had its day. This is the prototype, G-ADIF, being demonstrated by Chris Staniland only weeks before the aircraft was lost at Evère in July 1935. (*Aeroplane*)

Fox VII and VIII

Development
The last two marks of the successful, in Belgian service at least, Fairey Fox family, were the Mk VII and VIII. While the former was little more than an experimental conversion, the latter, alongside its predecessors, briefly saw action during Germany's onslaught in May 1940.

Design
The Fox VII evolved from the Mk VI but was designed as a single-seater, which was merely a temporary conversion as it could be put back to its original two-seater arrangement within hours. Armament was up to a maximum of six guns, four in the upper wings and two in the fuselage. As with the Fantôme, the Fox VII could be fitted with a 20mm Oerlikon moteur cannon if a Hispano-Suiza 12 Ycrs engine was installed instead of the two fuselage-mounted machine guns. The Fox VII was also referred to as the 'Mono-Fox' and, unofficially, as the 'Kangourou'; the latter coming about because of the way the large ventral radiator resembled a Kangaroo's pouch. The Fox VIII was also a modified and revised Mk VI, and it was fitted with a Ratier three-blade propeller instead of a wooden two-blade one.

Operational service
The first of only two Fox VIIs built first flew on 14 December 1935 from Gosselies, with Belgian test pilot A. J. Eyskens at the controls. The Fox VIII, of which 12 were ordered at the time of the Munich crisis in 1938, entered service in mid-1939, the last of them leaving the Gosselies production line on 25 May. The Fox VIII only served with 7/III/3, 7e Escadrille 'Flèche Ailée' at Evère during peacetime, and Belcele when World War Two began. It can only be presumed that the type did not serve beyond May 1940.

Production
Two Fox VIIs were built and only referred to as AF.6134 and AF.6142, and 12 Fox VIIIs were built without Avions Fairey construction numbers applied, but they were serialled as O–182 to O–193 in Belgian Air Force service.

Technical data - Fox VII and VIII	
ENGINE	(VII) One 860hp Hispano-Suiza 12 Ydrs or Ycrs
WINGSPAN	38ft
LENGTH	29ft 8in
HEIGHT	11ft
MAX SPEED	208mph at sea level
CLIMB	16,400ft in 7mins
CEILING	37,720ft

Fairey Fox VII AF.6134, one of only two of this mark ever built, was also known as the 'Mono-Fox' and the 'Kangourou'; a reference to the large pouch-like radiator under the fuselage. (Via Martyn Chorlton)

Fairey Fox VII. (Key Archive)

Battle

Development
When the specification for a new light bomber was issued in 1932, the world was a comparatively peaceful place. But as the 1930s progressed, it became clear that aircraft development and tactics were both rapidly advancing and improving at a pace much quicker than the Fairey Battle. Adequate when it entered service in 1937, it was hopelessly outclassed by the beginning of World War Two and was equally let down by being employed in the wrong theatre of action and with outdated tactics.

The aircraft was created in response to Air Ministry Specification P.27/32; originally issued in August 1932 but not confirmed until April 1933. The remit was that the aircraft should be in service by 1936, be able to a carry a bomb load of no less than 1,000lbs over a range of 1,000 miles and have a speed of no less than 200mph.

Design
Designed by Marcel Lobelle, the P.27/32 was designed to accommodate the PV.12 engine (the prototype Rolls-Royce Merlin) which was not available until the spring of 1934. The wing, a cantilever design built in five sections, housed the retractable undercarriage and a pair of bomb traps in each side for up to four 250lb bombs. The centre-section of the wing was integral to the fuselage, while aft of the pilot's cockpit construction was semi-monocoque. Lobelle presented his design to the Air Ministry on 11 June 1934, and, seemingly impressed with what they saw, a contract for a single prototype was awarded.

It was not until November 1935 that Rolls-Royce delivered a Merlin C engine to Fairey, although by the time Chris Staniland flew the prototype P.27/32, K4303, on 10 March 1936, the powerplant was a 970hp Merlin G. However, senior staff was so impressed with the aircraft, even before its first flight, an order for 155 aircraft was placed in September 1935. Now named the Battle, it was with this 'G' engine that K4303 was delivered to the A&AEE in October 1936, where all the performance figures as per Specification P.27/32 were achieved.

Technical data – Battle	
ENGINE	One 1,030hp Rolls-Royce Merlin I 12-cylinder liquid-cooled in-line and, later, Merlin II, III and V
WINGSPAN	54ft
LENGTH	42ft 4in
HEIGHT	15ft 6in
WING AREA	422 sq ft
EMPTY WEIGHT	6,647lb
LOADED WEIGHT	10,792lb
MAX SPEED	210mph at sea level; 257mph at 15,000ft
CLIMB	5,000ft in 4mins 6secs
CEILING	25,000ft
RANGE	1,000 miles at 200mph and 16,000ft

Operational service

Because of Roll-Royce's preoccupation with refining the Merlin engine for the Hurricane and Spitfire, further delays meant that the Battle did not enter RAF service until May 1937. The first recipient was 63 Squadron at Upwood, followed by 105 Squadron at Harwell, and, by the end of the year, five squadrons had converted to the Battle.

These early arrivals were all powered by the Merlin I, which proved a troublesome engine, and, after the 136th Battle was built, the unit was changed for the Merlin II, which caused a great deal conflict with Hurricane production at the time.

By the beginning of World War Two, 15 squadrons were equipped with the Battle, and, as part of the Advanced Air Striking Force (AASF) in support of the British Expeditionary Force (BEF), 12, 15, 40, 88, 103, 142, 150, 218 and 226 squadrons were all sent to France. The type's baptism of fire came during May 1940, when the light bomber was employed on a host of near suicidal low-level daylight attacks. One of these famous raids was on 12 May against the Meuse Bridge, Maastricht, when four out of five Battles from 12 Squadron failed to return, one of the crews being posthumously awarded the RAF's first Victoria Crosses for the determined attack. Virtually relegated to second-line duties on its return to England, the Battle saw out its operational days with 98 Squadron in July 1941.

Production

In total, 2,200 Battles were built, 1,171 of them by Fairey at Hayes and Heaton Chapel and 1,029 by Austin. 16 were supplied to Belgium, and, out of the grand total, 739 were shipped to Canada and 364 to Australia.

Right: The prototype P.27/32 (later Battle) is being demonstrated by Fairey test pilot Chris Staniland in April 1936. The aircraft was retired after 182.10 flying hours and saw out its days as an instructional airframe at 5 SoTT Locking from May 1939. (*Aeroplane*)

Below: A large number of Battles were converted to target-tugs, including ex-Battle I L5664, pictured here during trials with the A&AEE on 8 December 1941. The aircraft was later shipped to South Africa in June 1942. (Via Martyn Chorlton)

Seafox

Development
The Fairey Seafox was specifically designed to be launched from Royal Navy light cruisers and, as such, was designed to a very stringent specification. The specification, S.11/32, called for a two-seat reconnaissance floatplane, which would inevitably result in a lightly loaded, conventional aircraft.

Design
Of all-metal construction with fabric covered wings (which could be folded), the Seafox had a monocoque fuselage, which was made up of 'Z' sections covered in Alclad panelling. The pilot's cockpit was open, while the observer/gunner's station was covered in a transparent hood. The reason for the open cockpit was that the pilot had a better view during a catapult launch and, more importantly, a good view during recovery back to the ship. The enclosed canopy could be raised from the rear, allowing sufficient room for a Lewis machine-gun, which was fitted on a Fairey high-speed mount.

Originally designed to take a 500hp Bristol Aquila radial, which would have given the Seafox spirited performance, the unique 393hp Napier Rapier was selected instead. This one-off engine in military service initially suffered from excessive oil consumption and high cylinder head temperatures. These faults were eventually cured, but performance of the Seafox suffered as a result. The first of two prototypes, K4304, made its maiden flight from Hamble on 27 May 1936, and the second, K4305, which was built as a landplane, first flew on 5 November 1936, also by Hamble.

Operational service
After the Seafox had completed many trials and catapult tests with the RAE, and further trials with HMS *Neptune* off Gibraltar in March 1937, the Seafox entered service. The type served with 702, 713, 714, 716 and 718 Catapult Flights (all of these were later pooled into 700 Squadron from January 1940) and 703, 754, 764, 765 and 773 squadrons.

Technical data – Seafox	
ENGINE	One 395hp Napier Rapier VI 16-cylinder–H air-cooled
WINGSPAN	40ft
LENGTH	33ft 5in
HEIGHT	12ft 2in
WING AREA	434 sq ft
EMPTY WEIGHT	3,805lb
LOADED WEIGHT	5,420lb
MAX SPEED	124mph at 5,860ft
CRUISING SPEED	106mph
CLIMB	5,000ft in 15mins 30secs
CEILING	9,700ft
ENDURANCE	4.25hrs
RANGE	440 miles

The Seafox had an active service career up to its retirement from the FAA in 1943, the most distinguished action being its involvement in the Battle of the River Plate in December 1939. After an engagement with the *Admiral Graf Spee*, the Walruses on board HMS *Exeter* were damaged, leaving only one Seafox available on board HMS *Ajax*; a second Seafox had been destroyed. Flown by Lieutenant E. D. G. Lewin, with observer Lieutenant R. E. N. Kearney, the Seafox acted as a spotter for the guns of HMS *Ajax*, *Achilles* and *Exeter* throughout the action, and, on 17 December, was the first to report that *Graf Spee* had been scuttled off Montevideo. Lewin was later awarded the Distinguished Flying Cross for his part in the sinking of the *Graf Spee*; the first FAA officer to be decorated during World War Two.

Production

Sixty-six Seafoxes were built in 1936 and 1937, including two prototypes, K4304 and K4305. The first production batch of 49 aircraft was placed in January 1936, serialled K8569 to K8617, and a final repeat order of 15 aircraft ordered in September 1936, serialled L4519 to L4533.

Above: K8575, the seventh production Fairey Seafox, is captured taxiing in the Solent during flight testing in early July 1937. On 13 July, the aircraft was delivered to the FAA Pool at Lee-on-Solent. (*Aeroplane*)

Right: Seafox K8577 of 716 Flight is on board the Leander-class light cruiser, HMS *Neptune*, pictured before the ship left for South Africa in September 1937. The Seafox, which was being flown by Lieutenant D. H. Burke and Lieutenant J. Roe, was credited with spotting the German merchant ship *Inn*, which was sunk by gunfire on 5 September 1939. (*Aeroplane*)

P.4/34

Development
The aircraft that would later be known as the Fulmar was originally designed as a day bomber to Specification P.4/34, from which the two prototypes were named. Marcel Lobelle designed an aircraft that was very clean and very fast for a day bomber, and the machine inadvertently became the main contender for new Naval Specification O.8/38 for a carrier-borne fighter and observation aircraft. The caveat to this specification was that it would have to be a two-seater, because navigational aids that were efficient enough to get a lone pilot back to an aircraft carrier in open seas were still lacking in the late 1930s.

Design
Issued on 12 November 1934, Specification P.4/34 was also contended by Hawker's Henley, while Lobelle based Fairey's entrant on the Battle. The Fairey P.4/34 was lighter, smaller and improvements included an undercarriage which folded inwards and, unlike the Battle, retracted completely into the wing. The P.4/34 was also sufficiently stressed for dive-bombing duties, a level of strength that would stand it in good stead as a fighter in the future. Compared to the Henley, the Fairey P.3/34 carried its bombload externally, which was one of the main reasons why the Hawker aircraft won the original specification. However, the day-bomber requirement was later abandoned, leaving the Henley to serve out its days as a target-tug, while the P.4/34, in the guise of the Fulmar, was destined for a more action-packed career.

Operational service
The first of two prototypes, K5099 (c/n F.2231), was first flown on 13 January 1937, followed by the second P.4/24, K7555, on 19 April, both aircraft being flown by Chris Staniland. The latter would basically evolve as a flying mock-up of the Fulmar fleet-fighter from March 1938. Some of the modifications carried out to meet the specification included a reduction of 8in in the wingspan and repositioning of the tailplane 8in higher. K7555 was then delivered to Martlesham Heath, where it was tested during September and October 1937. The report was generally good, but the P.4/34 was let down by its stalling characteristics and heavy rudder control above 80mph. Following further modifications, the aircraft's behaviour during the stall was described as benign, and the rudder control was rectified by a bias control.

Technical data – P.4/34	
ENGINE	One 1,030hp Rolls-Royce Merlin I vee-12 liquid cooled
WINGSPAN	46ft 4½in
LENGTH	40ft
HEIGHT	14ft 1in
WING AREA	342 sq ft
EMPTY WEIGHT	6,405lb
LOADED WEIGHT	8,787lb
MAX SPEED	(Merlin II) 283mph at 15,000ft
MAX RATE OF CLIMB	1,200 ft/min
CEILING	26,600ft
RANGE	1,000 miles

The P.4/34 proved a useful test bed for other Fairey types as well, including the Firefly. K7555 was fitted with Fairey-Youngman flaps, which were tested by the RAE during 1941, and the future Fireflies' four-cannon installation was also trialled by the P.4/34. K7555 was also used to test pneumatically operated bellow-type air brakes. The first aircraft, K5099, also carried out its fair share of performance trials with the A&AEE and the RAE. It was with the latter that the aircraft was used for 'survival' tests in the event of a collision with barrage-balloon cables during mid-1937, followed by a variety of 'defence experiments'. The aircraft saw out its days as instructional airframe No.3665M. K7555 continued to serve Fairey and the RAE throughout the war and was not struck off charge until 18 March 1945.

The second P.4/34, K7555, gave valuable service, not only in support of the Fulmar, but also the Firefly; the aircraft served from April 1937 through to early 1945. (*Aeroplane*)

One of the more obvious differences between the Battle and the P.4/34 was the wide-track undercarriage, which retracted inwards instead of backwards and was completely concealed in a neat recess in the underside of the wing. (*Aeroplane*)

Albacore

Development

It is common knowledge that the Swordfish, which the Albacore was meant to replace, continued in service much longer than planned. The more refined Albacore was a classic example of an obsolete idea being over-developed. Refinements over its predecessor included a fully enclosed centrally heated cockpit, a windscreen wiper, a laboratory system, an automatic dinghy launching system, variable pitch propeller and hydraulically operated flaps. While this did make the Albacore a considerably more comfortable and efficient aircraft compared to the Swordfish, the concept had already been passed and had been successfully achieved by the older open-cockpit Fairey design.

Design

The Albacore was created from Specification M.7/36, dated September 1936, which called for a torpedo/bomber/reconnaissance aircraft with a speed range of between 58 and 183kts and the ability to carry an 18in Mk XIIA torpedo. Other criteria were dual-controls, a power-operated rear turret, full navigation and observation facilities plus sufficient heating and sound-proofing. M.7/36 was actually abandoned by the Air Ministry, but Fairey had already thrown itself into the specification and a new one was created, S.41/36, specifically for a Swordfish replacement, and the Albacore was the only competitor.

Designer Marcel Lobelle presented the ministry with two layouts to S.41/36, one a monoplane and the other a biplane. The monoplane was dismissed, so the Albacore became an equal-span, single-bay, folding-wing all-metal biplane, complete with a monocoque fuselage, fabric-covered wings, an enclosed twin cockpit and a heavily faired split undercarriage. Hydraulically operated flaps doubled as airbrakes when the aircraft was used for dive-bombing.

A Taurus II engine was initially fitted, later to be replaced by the more powerful Taurus XII. Armament was a single forward-firing machine gun in the upper starboard wing and one or two Vickers K machine-guns in the rear cockpit. As per the original specification, the Albacore could carry a single 18in 1,600lb torpedo or up to four 500lb bombs carried on racks under each lower wing.

Technical data – Albacore torpedo-bomber and reconnaissance	
ENGINE	One 1,065hp Bristol Taurus II 14-cylinder two-row sleeve-valve radial and later, one 1,130hp Taurus XII
WINGSPAN	50ft
LENGTH	(Land) 39ft 10in; (Sea) 42ft 5½in
HEIGHT	(Land) 14ft 2in; (Sea) 17ft 9in
WING AREA	623 sq ft
EMPTY WEIGHT	(TB) 7,250lb; (recce) 7,200lb
LOADED WEIGHT	(TB) 10,460lb; (recce) 9,615lb
MAX SPEED	(TB) 161mph at 4,500ft; (recce) 169mph at 4,500ft
CRUISING SPEED	116mph
CLIMB	6,000ft in 8mins
CEILING	20,700ft
RANGE	930 miles with a 1,610lb war load

Operational service

The prototype, L7074, was first flown from the Great West aerodrome by F. H. Dixon on 18 December 1939. This aircraft, and the second prototype, L7075, were not individually ordered but were the first pair from an initial production order of 100 aircraft. 826 Squadron, which was formed at RNAS Ford on 15 March 1940, was the first unit to receive the Albacore. This unit was also the first to take the type into action during the German invasion of the Low Countries, with the Albacores attacking E-boats off Zeebrugge and communication lines at Westende.

826 and 829 squadrons were the first Albacore units to embark on an aircraft carrier, when both joined HMS *Formidable* on 26 November 1940. Both of these units went on to serve with distinction in the Battle of Cape Matapan in March 1941. By 1942 and into mid-1943, the Albacore was already being superseded by another Fairey dive-bomber, the Barracuda, and, by November 1943, only 820 and 841 squadrons were still operating the type.

Production

All 800 Albacores were built at Hayes between 1938 and 1942. The type not only served with 46 FAA squadrons (16 of these were operational units), but also the RAF, the RCAF and RCN.

Albacore I of 786 Squadron, coded No.4, pictured on a clear day above the rolling hills of Fife, not far from its home airfield of Crail. (*Aeroplane*)

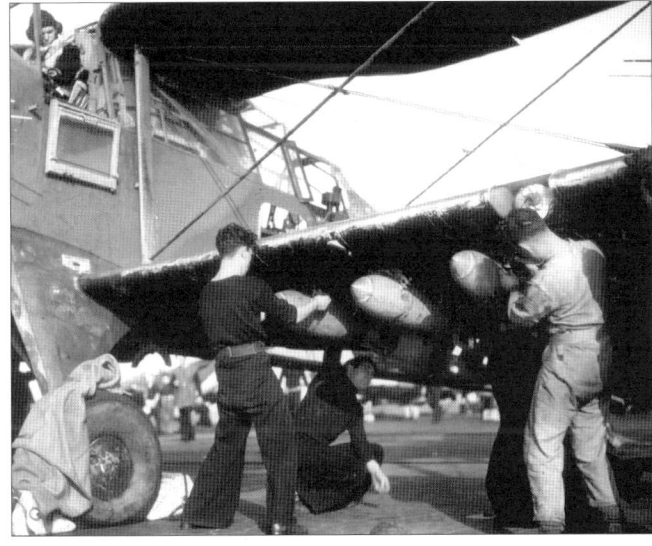

An Albacore being loaded with 250lb bombs on board HMS *Formidable* during Operation *Torch* in November 1942. (Via Martyn Chorlton)

F.C.1

Development

Concern was raised in 1938 by the Directorate of Civil Aviation about how far Britain was lagging behind in the development and production of civilian landplanes. The Douglas DC-2 and DC-3 were already beginning to dominate the world market, and, after many meetings, discussions and study groups, it was decided that financial aid was the only way to kick-start manufacturers into producing such aircraft.

At the same time, a pair of specifications was issued; 15/28 for a short to medium-haul aircraft in May 1938, and 14/38 for a long-haul transport, the latter being made public in July 1938. Short Brothers won the long-haul contract, while 14/38 saw a more hotly contested competition, with Armstrong Whitworth, Bristol, Fairey, General Aircraft and Vickers all receiving requests to tender. Later, Folland also became involved but, after much negotiation, only Fairey remained – the only manufacturer which had not been seriously involved in civilian aircraft before.

Design

By October 1938, Fairey estimated that the cost of a pair of prototypes, minus engines, would be £385,000, and if 12 aircraft were ordered into production, an estimated maximum cost of £80,000 each was quoted. Once treasury approval was received, Fairey formally announced that it would start work on the F.C.1 (Fairey Commercial Number One) which, following an agreement of 12 November 1938, would serve with British Airways.

The F.C.1 was designed as a four-engine aircraft, mainly because the 15/38 requirements for take-off distance meant that there were not two engines available at the time with sufficient power should one fail. The aircraft was to have a pressurised cabin capable of carrying 26 passengers (plus four more occasional) with a crew of five. The aircraft had a tricycle undercarriage, and, to give it excellent short-field landing and take-off performance, the F.C.1 was fitted with Fairey-Youngman flaps. Power was to be provided by four 1,000hp Taurus engines on the prototype and the untried 1,200hp Exe (Boreas) for the production.

By the spring of 1939, a very complex mock-up had been built, and an equally detailed model was being wind tunnel tested, by which time, an official production order had been placed. Unfortunately, World War Two got in the way, and, on 17 October 1939, the F.C.1 was cancelled, and one month later Specification 14/38 was also cancelled. Following the end of World War Two, it is alleged that Fairey seriously considered reviving the F.C.1, taking advantage of its wartime production lines and a large number of employees. Planned with Bristol Hercules engines, up to three prototypes were planned with sufficient tooling to produce up to 200 aircraft.

F.C.1

Technical data – F.C.1	
ENGINE	(Prototype) Four 1,000hp Bristol Taurus 14-cylinder sleeve-valve radial; (Production) Four 1,200hp Rolls-Royce Exe 24-cylinder X sleeve-valve pressure air-cooled
WINGSPAN	105ft
LENGTH	82ft
WING AREA	1,300 sq ft
LOADED WEIGHT	(short-haul) 42,000lb
MAX SPEED	275mph at 13,000ft
STALLING SPEED	70mph
MAX RANGE IN STILL AIR	1,700 miles at 50 per cent rated power

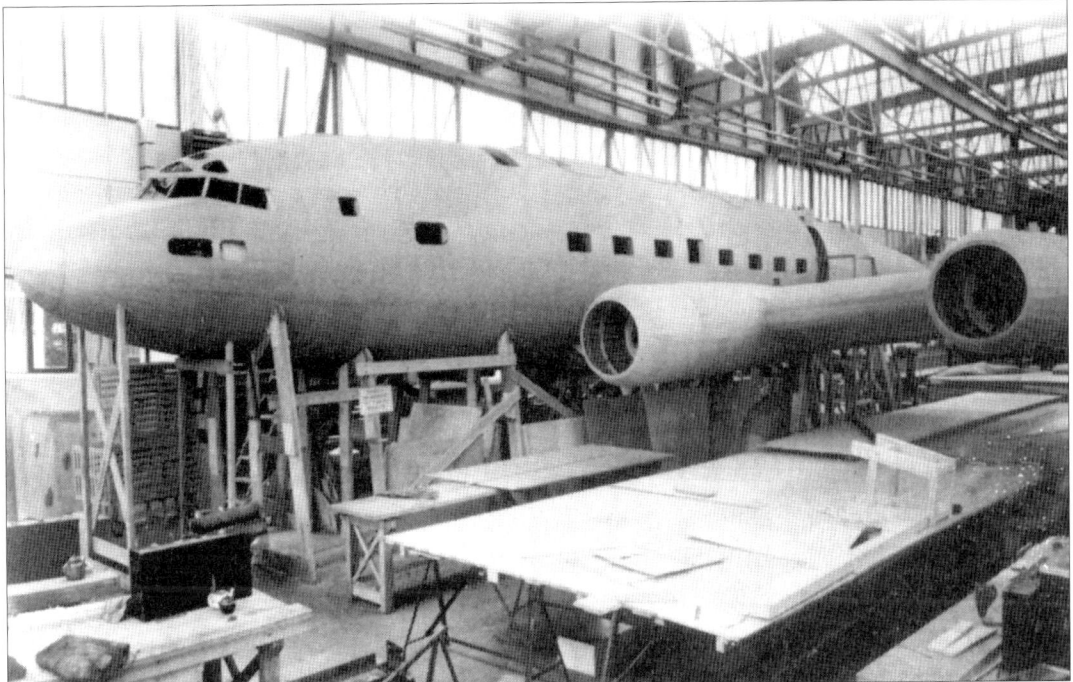

The F.C.1 only managed to reach an advanced mock-up stage before it was cancelled in October 1939. This is the mock-up in the Hayes experimental shops in the spring of 1939. (*Aeroplane*)

Primer Trainer

Development
Prior to the beginning of World War Two, the Avions Fairey's designer, Ernest O. Tips, had created the moderately successful range of Tipsy aircraft. This included the Tipsy S single-seater and the Tipsy B two-seater, the latter being developed during the post-war period. Another Tipsy machine was the Primary Trainer, or Tipsy M, later renamed the Primer Trainer, which was taken over by Fairey in 1948 with the intention of beginning limited production at Hamble. The origins of this aircraft were in the prototype, OO-POM, originally designated as the Tipsy M in 1938. This aircraft was dismantled and secretly shipped to England prior to the German invasion of Belgium, although the aircraft had previously been tested by Fairey pilots in June 1939. Once reassembled, the Tipsy M was recorded as flying from the Great West aerodrome between November 1940 and May 1941, and again until September as a company communications aircraft. Dismantled and stored again, the aircraft would not appear again until the war was over.

Design
A low-wing monoplane, the Fairey Primer Trainer had a fully enclosed tandem cockpit and was powered by a Gipsy Major 10 engine. The aircraft had manually operated flaps and a fixed undercarriage, which, on OO-POM (by now re-registered as G-AKSK but flown displaying 'G-6-1'), was spatted and fitted with wheel brakes. The fuselage and sections of the wing were constructed from bronze-welded metal tubes backed up by the subsidiary components made of wood, such as the stringers and ribs. The Primer was fabric-covered.

Operational service
As soon as the war was over, OO-POM was returned to Avions Fairey, where some minor modifications were carried out before the aircraft was taken over by Fairey in 1947. Ex-OO-POM was registered as G-AKSK in February 1948 and, not long after, was delivered to the A&AEE at Boscombe Down for flight testing and various assessments. The aircraft was then dismantled again at Hayes so that production drawings could be produced, and a set of jigs were designed and assembled. The original drawings and technical information had been deliberately destroyed by staff of Avions Fairey in 1940. The first production aircraft, registered as G-ALBL 'G-6-4', was made up of parts of G-AKSK, including the Major engine. G-ALBL was certificated on 22 October 1948 and, during its brief flying career, the Major was replaced by a Cirrus Major only for the aircraft to be dismantled in 1949. The second production aircraft, G-ALEW 'G-6-5', was fitted with the 155hp Cirrus Major engine and was put forward as a primary trainer for the RAF in competition with the de Havilland Canada Chipmunk. Having failed to secure this potentially huge military contract, the last Primer was dismantled in 1951. G-AKSK is recorded as having been sold abroad in August 1948, but to where, and whether the Primer was in an airworthy condition, is not known.

Production
Three aircraft were produced, ex-OO-POM (re-registered as G-AKSK), G-ALBL (c/n F.8455) and G-ALEW (c/n F.8456).

Technical data – Primer	
ENGINE	One 145hp Gipsy Major 10 four-cylinder inline air-cooled; or a 155hp Blackburn Cirrus Major 3
WINGSPAN	32ft 10in
LENGTH	27ft 6in
HEIGHT	6ft 10in
WING AREA	154.5 sq ft
EMPTY WEIGHT	1,360lb
LOADED WEIGHT	1,960lb
MAX SPEED	134mph at sea level
CRUISING SPEED	122mph
STALLING SPEED	(flaps down) 51mph
CEILING	19,500ft
CRUSING RANGE	383 miles

The original Tipsy M trainer, OO-POM, which served as the prototype Fairey Primer Trainer and was later re-registered G-AKSK, is pictured out of White Waltham in early 1948. (Charles E. Brown via Martyn Chorlton)

Fulmar I and II

Development

The Fulmar was able to hit the ground running because of all the valuable work already achieved by the P.4/34, and, as such, no further prototype was needed. The first Fulmar to fly was a production aircraft from an initial batch of 40 aircraft, of which two of this group were planned as seaplanes. However, by March 1939, a decision to use the Fulmar in this role was dropped. The actual name Fulmar was not applied to the aircraft until August 1938, and the type was not officially made public until after it had joined the FAA in June 1940.

The very first production Fulmar, N1854, was flown for the first time by Duncan Menzies from Ringway on 4 January 1940. After being sent to the A&AEE, along with N1855 and N1858, and then to HMS *Illustrious* for further trials, N1854 was retained by Fairey for development work. Later converted to Mk II standard with a Merlin 30 engine, the aircraft remained airworthy into the post-war period and was re-registered as G-AIBE. The Fulmar served as a hack and general communications aircraft until it was finally retired on 18 December 1962; today it is preserved in the FAA Museum at Yeovilton.

The Fulmar II was fitted with the Merlin 30 engine, and, as a result, several modifications had to be made. These included a Rotol propeller, new radiator, oil cooler, a revised sump for the fuel tank, bigger pipes for the fuel system, trimmer stops and a rudder mass-balance. The first production Fulmar II, N4021, made its maiden flight from Ringway on 20 January 1941.

Operational service

The Fulmar first went into action in September 1940 during the protection of the Malta convoys. The opposition at the time was the Italian Air Force, and the combined efforts of 806, 807 and 808 squadrons sent many enemy aircraft plunging into the Mediterranean. The Fulmars of 806 Squadron were particularly successful and, during November alone, shot down six more enemy aircraft whilst providing fighter cover for the Swordfish operation at Taranto.

Technical data – Fulmar I and II	
ENGINE	One 1,080hp Merlin VIII 12-cylinder liquid-cooled and later one 1,300hp Merlin 30
WINGSPAN	46ft 4½in
LENGTH	40ft 3in
HEIGHT	14ft
WING AREA	342 sq ft
EMPTY WEIGHT	(I) 6,915lb; (II) 7,015lb
LOADED WEIGHT	(I) 9,800lb; (II) 9,672lb
MAX SPEED	(I) 280mph (II) 272mph
CRUISING SPEED	235mph
MAX RATE OF CLIMB	1,200 ft/min
CEILING	(I) 26,000ft (II) 27,200ft
RANGE	(I) 800 miles (II) 780 miles

The Fulmar also played a vital role during the Petsamo attack in July 1941, and convoy protection for the Russian convoys, the siege of Malta and both the North African and subsequent Italian invasions. The type also helped to shadow the *Bismarck* in May 1941 and was used for night-intruder operations as the NF.II, night-fighter training and even target towing as the TT.II. The Fulmar served with a total of 49 FAA squadrons (and one RAF unit, 273 Squadron), 18 of which were operational units on board eight fleet aircraft carriers and five escort carriers until 8 February 1945.

Production

A total of 600 Fulmar Is and IIs were built; 250 were Mk Is and 350 were Mk IIs. The Fulmar was produced between 1940 and 1943; peak production was 319 aircraft in 1941.

The first production Merlin 30-powered Fulmar II, N4021, first flew in January 1941. This photograph was taken on 2 June 1942 whilst undergoing testing with the A&AEE at Boscombe Down. (*Aeroplane*)

The Fairey Fulmar entered FAA service in 1940, and, despite being overtaken by the better equipped and more powerful single-seat machines from 1943 onwards, the type remained operational until early 1945. (Charles E. Brown via Martyn Chorlton)

Barracuda I

Development

Another creation from the drawing board of Marcel Lobelle, the Barracuda was designed to replace the Albacore in the torpedo carrying role, but by the time the aircraft entered service, the 'mighty metal monster' (as dubbed by the FAA) also brought the art of dive bombing back into FAA operations. A continuation of the Battle, Fulmar and Firefly train of thought, the Fairey Barracuda was designed, built and flown in the space of 20 months but was stalled when demand for its powerplant, the Rolls-Royce Merlin, was being diverted to the Spitfire and Hurricane. Designed to Specification S.24/27, dating from November 1937, a contract for two prototypes was not placed until January 1939, and, by August, a production contract was in place.

Design

The Barracuda had a high-set shoulder wing, all-metal stressed skin fuselage and a long canopy that enclosed the pilots, observer/navigators and wireless operator air/gunners. Because of the shoulder wing, the undercarriage was hinged at the base of the fuselage, retracting outboard into the wing roots. Another novel feature of the aircraft was the fitment of Fairey-Youngman flaps mounted above and below the trailing edge of the wing. These provided lift on take-off, a larger area wing in flight and drag during landing as well as providing stability during a dive-bombing attack.

The first prototype had a conventional tailplane but, during early test flights, it was found that when the Youngman flaps were set at a negative angle (during a 30 degrees dive-bombing attack), the wake from them caused severe tailplane buffet. The solution was to mount the tailplane high on the fin in a 'T-tail' arrangement, which was strut braced for added strength. Power was originally intended to be the Rolls-Royce 1,200hp Exe, but when development was abandoned, the 1,300hp Merlin 30 was chosen instead.

Technical data – Barracuda I	
ENGINE	One 1,300hp Rolls-Royce Merlin 30 twelve-cylinder vee liquid-cooled
WINGSPAN	49ft 2in; (folded) 17ft 9in
LENGTH	39ft 9in
HEIGHT	15ft 2in
WING AREA	405 sq ft
EMPTY WEIGHT	8,700lb
MAX LOADED WEIGHT	13,500lb
MAX SPEED	235mph at 11,000ft
MAX CRUISING SPEED	191mph at 6,000ft
CLIMB	6,000ft in 6.7 min
CEILING	18,400ft
RANGE	853 miles with a 1,610lb torpedo

Operational service

The first aircraft, P1767, was flown on its maiden flight by Chris Staniland from the Great West aerodrome on 7 December 1940, followed by the second Barracuda, P1770 on 29 June 1941. The Barracuda I entered service with 785 and 786 squadrons at Crail and 831 Squadron at Lee-on-Solent in December 1942. The Mk I also served with 747, 767, 768, 778, 787 and 827 squadrons, but with regard to the two operational units, the Barracuda I never saw any action. It remained in FAA service until August 1944 when it was withdrawn from the strength of 767 Squadron at East Haven.

Production

32 Barracuda Is were built including the two prototypes, P1767 (c/n F.4468) and P1770 (c/n F.4469). Both prototypes and P9642 to P9666 (25) were built at Hayes and five aircraft, DN625 to DN629 built by Westlands.

The prototype Barracuda I, P1767 (c/n F.4468), was first flown from the Great West aerodrome by Chris Staniland on 7 December 1940. The aircraft is pictured after the tailplane was repositioned to the high-fin position that would be one of the many distinctive features of the Barracuda. (*Aeroplane*)

An unusual pose for a Barracuda carrying a torpedo which the type as whole was never destined to drop in anger. However, the aircraft did reintroduce the art of dive-bombing back to FAA operations, a role in which the type was generally successful. (*Aeroplane*)

Swordfish II, III and IV

Design
The design of the Swordfish II, III and IV differed little from the Swordfish I. Introduced into production by Blackburn in 1941, the Mk II was the most prolifically built of all Swordfish. The most significant difference from the earlier mark was that, from the Mk II onwards, the underside of the lower wing was strengthened with a metal skin, enabling the aircraft to carry up to eight 60lb RPs. It was this very effective, yet simple weapon that was tested by a Swordfish at the A&AEE during 1941 for the first time.

The original 690hp Pegasus powered many early Swordfish Mk IIs, but this was later replaced by the 750hp Pegasus 30, which was installed in all later aircraft, including all Mk IIIs and Mk IVs. The Swordfish III had a strengthened lower wing but was also modified to carry an ASV (Air-to-Surface-Vessel) Mk X radar inside a large radome mounted between the undercarriage legs. The Swordfish IV was basically a Mk II fitted with a fully enclosed canopy specifically for training use in Canada. Basic defensive armament was the same as the Swordfish I, and all later marks could also carry a single 18in torpedo, a 1,500lb sea mine or the same weight in bombs and depth charges. Because of the strengthened wing, as well as the eight RPs, the Mk II and III could alternatively carry eight 25lb armour-piercing RPs on the same under-wing rails. The Mk III also had the option of being fitted with rocket-assisted take-off gear (RATOG) which was designed for Swordfish operations with heavy loads from short decks, such as escort carriers and MAC ships. Several Swordfish were also modified to accept a Leigh Light under the port wing for nocturnal submarine hunting.

Operational service
The Swordfish II entered FAA service in 1941 and the Mk III in 1943; both continuing to serve until mid-1946. The Swordfish II served with a remarkable 64 FAA squadrons, 23 of them operational. The Swordfish Mk III served with 20 different FAA squadrons, and, between the two marks, the type served at sea aboard HMS *Argus, Ark Royal, Courageous, Eagle, Furious, Glorious, Hermes, Illustrious, Indefatigable* and *Victorious*. The MAC ships and escort carriers including HMS *Activity, Archer,*

Technical data – Swordfish II and III landplane	
ENGINE	One 690hp Bristol Pegasus IIIM3 nine-cylinder radial and later one 750hp Pegasus 30
WINGSPAN	45ft 6in
LENGTH	35ft 8in
HEIGHT	12ft 4in
WING AREA	607 sq ft
EMPTY WEIGHT	4,700lb
LOADED WEIGHT	6,750lb
MAX SPEED	(Torpedo bomber) 139mph at 4,750ft
CRUISING SPEED	104–129mph at 5,000ft
CLIMB RATE	(III) 5,000ft in 10 mins
RANGE	(Normal fuel and 1,610lb torpedo) 546 miles

Attacker, Avenger, Battler, Biter, Campania, Chaser, Dasher, Fencer, Hunter, Nairana, Rapana, Stalker, Tracker and *Vindex* were also frequented by Swordfish IIs and IIIs.

Production

All production of the Swordfish II, III and the Mk IV conversions was carried out by the Blackburn Aircraft Company at Sherburn in Elmet, North Yorkshire. This equated to 1,080 Mk IIs and 320 Mk IIIs. In total, 110 Mk IIs were converted to Mk IVs, and Blackburn also supplied the Royal Canadian Navy with 99 Mk IIs and six Mk IIIs.

Right: The venerable Swordfish II, LS326, of the RNHF, first entered FAA service in August 1943. This popular airshow performer has received a great deal of attention over recent years, which will hopefully see the aircraft remain airworthy for a long time to come. (Via Martyn Chorlton)

Below: In total, 110 Swordfish IIs were modified with canopies over the cockpits for training in Canada. Referred to as the Mk IV, there is no actual official evidence from the period when this designation was used. (Via Martyn Chorlton)

Firefly F.1 (including FR and NF.1/2)

Development
Created from a requirement that had its seeds sown in the 1920s, the Firefly was the latest in a long line of two-seat spotter-reconnaissance aircraft, whose performance was good enough for it to be classed as a fighter. By the time the Firefly arrived, more emphasis had been placed on the fighter role, but the aircraft would evolve into many specialist variants.

Design
Designed by H. E. Chaplin, the Firefly made full use of the Fairey-Youngman flap arrangement, although unlike the untidy arrangement of the Barracuda, these could be fully and neatly retracted into the wing. The Firefly F.1 was a two-seat observer-navigated day fighter, armed with four 20mm cannon and powered by a Griffon IIB engine, which gave the aircraft a top speed of 316mph at 14,000ft, which was more than 40mph faster than the Fulmar. The Mk I had a number of derivatives, beginning with the FR.1, which was fitted with ASH submarine and ship-detected radar mounted in a pod directly under the forward fuselage. Next was the NF.1, a night-fighter version of the FR.1, and the F.1A, which was a standard F.1 converted to an FR.1. Others were the T.1 dual trainer, the more radical converted post-war T.1 and the TT.1 target-tug (all covered in separate chapters). An anomaly was the NF.2, which was a derivative of the Mk I but was modified to such an extent that it warranted a different variant. The NF.2 was much heavier than previous aircraft because of the additional equipment needed for an AI operator, and because the centre of gravity was moved aft. To compensate for the latter, an 18in-long fuselage-lengthening bay was installed behind the engine firewall. Later, NF.2s were converted back to Mk I standard.

Operational service
The first of four prototypes/development aircraft, Z1826 was first flown by Chris Staniland on 22 December 1941 and then the second, Z1827, on 4 June 1942. Unfortunately, it was the latter aircraft

Technical data – Firefly F.I	
ENGINE	One 1,730hp Rolls-Royce Griffon IIB 12 cylinder vee liquid-cooled
WINGSPAN	44ft 6in; (folded) 13ft 6in
LENGTH	37ft 7in
HEIGHT	13ft 7in
WING AREA	328 sq ft
EMPTY WEIGHT	9,750lb
LOADED WEIGHT	14,020lb
MAX SPEED	316mph at 14,000ft
CLIMB	5,000ft in 2mins 30secs
CEILING	28,000ft
RANGE	1,300 miles

that claimed Staniland's life on 26 June, when the Firefly suffered an elevator over-balance that caused the tail-unit to fail at low level.

The first production aircraft was delivered to Yeovilton on 4 March 1943, and it was here that the first unit, 1770 Squadron, was formed with the type in October 1943. By the end of World War Two nine FAA squadrons were operating the Mk I or one of its sub-variants. The F.1/FR.1 served with a total of 48 FAA squadrons, the NF.1 with 12 squadrons and the NF.2 with two. Firefly Mk Is flew their first operational sortie in July 1944, when 1770 Squadron from HMS *Indefatigable* led a dive-bombing raid against the Tirpitz. The same unit also took part in the FAA's first major action against the Japanese in January 1945 when oil refineries in Sumatra were destroyed by an RP attack.

Production

By late 1946, 872 Mk Is had been built Fairey constructed. The following types were built at Hayes: 327 F.1s, 376 FR.1/NF.1s and 37 NF.2s. Meanwhile, General Aircraft built a further 132 Mk Is.

Above: Out of the 1,569 Fireflies built, 740 were Mk Is, including this aircraft, MB727, photographed by Charles E. Brown. (Charles E. Brown via *Aeroplane*)

Right: The third prototype Firefly, Z1828, which first flew on 26 August 1942, is pictured during trials aboard HMS *Illustrious* later in the year. (Via Martyn Chorlton)

Barracuda II

Design
The Barracuda II differed from the Mk I by being fitted with a 1,640hp Rolls-Royce Merlin 32, driving a four-blade propeller and having the ability to carry an ASV radar. The latter was a Mk IIN radar with Yagi-type antennae, which was fitted to each outer upper wing. By far the most prolific mark built, the Barracuda II, thanks to the extra horsepower of the Merlin 32, could carry a wide range of external stores. While the torpedo was never carried in anger, various bombs, depth charges and mines were, and at least one Mk II was fitted with an air sea rescue (ASR) lifeboat below the fuselage. Another aircraft had containers fitted under each wing, large enough to carry two paratroopers in each. Tested by the Airborne Forces Experimental Establishment, several successful 'live' drops were made, but the idea was abandoned when it was realised that the psychological effect on the paratroopers, because of being enclosed in such a small space for a long time, was too much to bear.

Operational service
The Barracuda II first entered FAA service when 12 aircraft were delivered to 827 Squadron at Stretton on 10 January 1943. However, the aircraft did not see any action until September 1943, while serving with 810 Squadron from HMS *Illustrious* during the Salerno landings. Two months later, *Illustrious* was joined by 847 Squadron before setting sail for Ceylon, where the Barracuda squadrons became part of the 21st TBR Wing. Employed generally for anti-shipping patrols, the aircraft were also used to attack the occasional shore target including oil storage tanks and docks at Sabang in Sumatra, and a Japanese submarine base during 1944.

The Mk II hit the headlines on 3 April 1944, when 831 Squadron aboard HMS *Furious* and 827, 829 and 830 squadrons aboard HMS *Victorious*, escorted by Wildcats, Seafires, Corsairs and Hellcats, attacked the battleship Tirpitz at Kåfjord in Northern Norway. Attacking in two waves, the Barracudas managed to score up to 15 direct hits with 500lb SAPs and 1,000lb HEs, causing sufficient damage to keep the battleship in Kåfjord for repairs into the summer of 1944. Only three Barracudas and a single

Technical data – Barracuda II	
ENGINE	One 1,640hp Rolls-Royce Merlin 32 12-cylinder liquid-cooled
WINGSPAN	49ft 2in; (folded) 17ft 9in
LENGTH	39ft 9in
HEIGHT	15ft 2in
WING AREA	405 sq ft
EMPTY WEIGHT	9,350lb
MAX LOADED WEIGHT	14,100lb
MAX SPEED	228mph at 1,750ft
CRUISING SPEED	193mph at 5,000ft
CLIMB	5,000ft in 6mins
CEILING	16,600ft
RANGE	686 miles with a 1,610lb torpedo

fighter were lost in this brave action, which was repeated in May and August 1944 but not with the same level of success. The Mk II served with 53 FAA squadrons, 20 of them operational, and also with the RAF's 567, 667, 679 and 691 squadrons; the type was withdrawn from service by the summer of 1945.

Production

In total, 1,688 Barracuda IIs were built: 675 by Fairey at its Stockport and Ringway factories, 700 by Blackburn, 300 by Boulton Paul and 13 by Westland.

Above: Barracuda II P9795 (F.4668) demonstrating a pair of paratroop containers during trials with the A&AEE. Each container, designed to carry two paratroops each, was fitted with portholes fore and aft on each side to reduce the effects of claustrophobia. (*Aeroplane*)

Right: Blackburn-built Mk II, MX613, was modified to carry a substantial ASR lifeboat, which apparently worked well but was only ever used for experiments and demonstrations. (*Aeroplane*)

Barracuda III (aka TR.III)

Design
First flown in 1943 following the conversion of Boulton Paul-built Mk II, DP855, the Barracuda III did not enter service until 1944. Specifically introduced for anti-submarine operations, the Mk III was fitted with an ASV Mk X (redesignated Mk XI) radar in an enclosed radome under the rear fuselage. This radar had a range of 38 miles when used against surface ships, and, when the conditions were right, a submarine on the surface could be detected from a distance of 12 miles. The weapon of choice for these operations was a single 1,500lb mine, which was carried on crutches underneath the fuselage.

Operational service
The Barracuda III, redesignated as the TR.III, first entered operational service with 815, 821 and 822 squadrons in January 1945 and 810 Squadron in the following month. Only 821 Squadron enjoyed a period of limited action, operating from HMS *Puncher* laying mines off the Norwegian coast. During these final months of the war, the squadron came and went across the North Sea, also serving with HMS *Campania*, *Puncher* and *Searcher* before embarking on HMS *Trumpeter*. In July 1945, it was bound for the Far East to join the Eastern Fleet. VJ Day arrived before it could make a difference and, in early September, the squadron returned home aboard HMS *Fencer* without aircraft, only to re-equip with new TR.IIIs at Rattray. By February 1946, 821 Squadron was disbanded, leaving 815 Squadron, which re-equipped with the TR.III for a second time in December 1947.

Mainly operating to and from Eglinton during this period, the unit did not relinquish its TR.IIIs until May 1953. In the second line, 750 Squadron kept the TR.III on strength until July 1953. 860 Squadron was the only other operational unit with the TR.III between January 1945 and January 1946, operating from Maydown, Ayr and Fearn. In the second line, the TR.III served 700, 703, 707, 710, 713, 714, 719, 735, 737, 744, 747, 750, 756, 769, 778, 783, 785, 796, 798 and 799 squadrons.

Technical data – Barracuda III	
ENGINE	One 1,640hp Rolls-Royce Merlin 30 12-cylinder vee liquid-cooled
WINGSPAN	49ft 2in; (folded) 17ft 9in
LENGTH	39ft 9in
HEIGHT	15ft 2in
WING AREA	405 sq ft
EMPTY WEIGHT	9,407lb
MAX LOADED WEIGHT	14,100lb
MAX SPEED	239mph at 1,750ft
CRUISING SPEED	205mph at 5,000ft
CLIMB	5,000ft in 4mins 30secs
CEILING	20,000ft
RANGE	684 miles with a 1,572lb torpedo

Production

In total, 852 Barracuda IIIs were built by Fairey and Boulton Paul. Fairey produced 406 in the serial ranges PM682 to PM999, PN115 to PN164 and RK328 to RK574. Boulton Paul built 392 in the serial ranges, MD811 to MD992, ME104 to ME293 and RJ759 to RJ966. A further 208 aircraft contracted to Boulton Paul were cancelled.

Barracuda TR.III MD892 'R3M' of 714 Squadron is pictured over the Irish Sea during a training exercise from Ronaldsway. (*Aeroplane*)

Devoid of squadron markings and its ASV Mk X radar, TR.III RJ905 of 750 Squadron warms its Merlin engine through at St Merryn in 1953. (Via Martyn Chorlton)

Barracuda V

Design

Although it appeared to be nothing more than a modified TR.III with a Griffon engine on the surface, the Barracuda V was, in fact, a very different animal compared to its predecessors. The aircraft was redesigned to serve in the war in the Pacific as an interim, pending the arrival of the Spearfish but was ultimately too late, never entering operational service and only being produced in small numbers. The prototype aircraft, which was designated the Mk IV, was converted to Mk II P9976, powered by a 1,850hp Griffon VII (later an VIII) engine. First flown on 16 November 1944, from Ringway by Flight Lieutenant S. M. Moseley, the aircraft was built for a crew of two, namely the pilot and a navigator/radar-operator.

The production aircraft were each powered by a 2,020hp Griffon 37, and amongst the many modifications were a redesigned wing with squared-off tips and a span 4ft longer than the earlier aircraft. The aircraft was structurally strengthened, the electrical systems were heavily modified and brought up to date, and a new radar scanner was fitted to the leading edge of the port inside a radome, which was easily removable as a single unit. A single forward firing machine gun was fitted and the fuel capacity of the Mk V was increased. The early production Mk Vs, later designated as TR.Vs, were Mk II and Mk III conversions that used the same fin and rudder, but, from RK530 onwards (the first proper production aircraft), a large dorsal fin was fitted complete with an increased area rudder, which rose to a point above the fin. The first production aircraft took to the air on 22 November 1945, and the last was delivered on 27 October 1947.

Operational Service

The Barracuda TR.V only served with two FAA units, both of which were second line. The first was 778 Squadron at Ford, the type remaining on strength from September 1946 to July 1947, and the second was 783 Squadron, based at Lee-on-Solent, from December 1947 to October 1948.

Production

Only 35 Barracuda TR.Vs were built from the original order for 140 aircraft, including ex-Mk IIs P9976, DT845, PM940, PM941 and PM944, all by Fairey in the serial ranges, RK530 to RK542 and RK558 to RK574.

Technical data – Barracuda V	
ENGINE	(Prototype) One 1,850hp Rolls-Royce Griffon VII 12 cylinder vee liquid-cooled; (Production) One 2,020hp Griffon 37
WINGSPAN	53ft; (folded) 18ft 5½in
LENGTH	41ft 7in
HEIGHT	17ft 3in
WING AREA	435 sq ft
EMPTY WEIGHT	11,430lb
NORMAL LOADED WEIGHT	15,250lb
MAX SPEED	253mph at 10,000ft
CLIMB	10,000ft in 8mins 36secs
CEILING	24,000ft
RANGE	600 miles at 163mph with 2,000lbs of bombs

The Rolls-Royce Griffon 37 engine fitted in the TR.V did nothing to improve the appearance of the Barracuda. This is RK532, pictured in October 1946. (*Aeroplane*)

Originally built by Fairey as a Mk II, P9976 was the original TR.V prototype and was powered by the Griffon VII engine. (Via Martyn Chorlton)

The final look of the Fairey Barracuda after almost six years of development. The potential of the TR.V was cut short by the end of World War Two. (*Aeroplane*)

Spearfish

Development
As early as January 1943, the Specification O.5/43 was issued for the replacement of the Barracuda and, ultimately, the Grumman Avenger, which entered FAA at a similar time. The American-built Avenger performed better than the Barracuda, mainly because its weapons load was carried internally, and the aircraft was lighter and the engine more powerful. Fairey attempted to design all of these factors into its latest aircraft, the Spearfish.

Design
Designed by Herbert Eugene Chapman, the Spearfish was heavily influenced by the fact that it was intended for the Royal Navy's new 45,000-ton Gibraltar-class fleet carriers, which were planned to be commissioned by 1945. These huge carriers gave Eugene the freedom to design an aircraft much larger than the Barracuda, and with the option of the new, powerful Bristol Centaurus engine, the Spearfish was destined to be a brute of an aircraft. The aircraft's size was partly dictated by a large weapons bay, capable of holding four 500lb bombs, a single 1,800lb, 18in torpedo and/or a combination of mines and depth charges. Defensive armament employed the .50in Browning machine gun; two forward-firing, and two in a remotely controlled Frazer Nash Type 95 in a barbette behind the rear cockpit.

As with the Barracuda before it, Fairey-Youngman flaps were employed, although, on the Spearfish, these were fully retractable. The Spearfish had hydraulically folding wings, a hydraulically powered sliding canopy, space for a Mk XV ASV radar inside a retractable radome below the rear fuselage, and a substantial, outwardly retracting undercarriage. The 2,585hp Centaurus 57 engine was flushly fitted into the nose of the Spearfish; for example, the exhaust manifolds were recessed, and the oil cooler was neatly installed into the port leading edge of the wing. The aircraft was fitted with a Rotol five-blade constant-speed propeller, but later-production aircraft were to be fitted with a reverse pitch propeller that could double as an airbrake during a diving attack.

Operational Service
The prototype, RA356, built at Hayes, was first flown on 5 July 1945 by Fairey's chief test pilot Flight Lieutenant Foster Hickman Dixon. Production was planned to be carried out at Fairey's Heaton Chapel factory in Stockport, and the first aircraft, RN241, left there on 29 December 1945. Eight prototypes were ordered, and an order for 152 production aircraft was already in place when news came through that the Gibraltar fleet carriers had been cancelled, and all FAA's requirements for torpedo-carrying aircraft were abandoned.

Regardless, work continued at a much slower rate on the two airframes, RA360 and RA363, which were still under construction at Hayes, while RN244 and TJ179 were eventually completed; neither was destined to fly. TJ175 was the last Spearfish to take to the air in September 1947 and is believed to have been the last one flying; the aircraft serving with the Royal Navy's Carrier Trials Unit at Ford until the summer of 1952.

Production
Eight prototypes were ordered: RA356, RA360, RA363, RN241, RN244, TJ175, TJ179 and TJ184. A total of 152 production aircraft were built, but the project was cancelled in 1945.

Technical data – Spearfish	
ENGINE	One 2,585hp Bristol Centaurus 57 14-cylinder air-cooled sleeve-valved radial
WINGSPAN	60ft 3in; (folded) 20ft
LENGTH	44ft 7in
HEIGHT	13ft 6in
EQUIPPED EMPTY WEIGHT	15,200lb
OVERLOAD WEIGHT	(bomber) 22,083lb; (long-range recce) 21,882lb
MAX SPEED	292mph at 14,000ft
CLIMB	10,000ft in 7mins 45secs
CEILING	25,000ft
MAX RANGE	1,036 miles at 196mph at 15,000ft

Right: The prototype Spearfish, RA356, which first flew in July 1945, was only ever used as an aerodynamic test aircraft with armament. (Via Martyn Chorlton)

Below: Hayes-built RA360, which first flew on 23 September 1947, presents a good view of how neatly the powerful Centaurus engine was fitted. (Via Martyn Chorlton)

Firefly 4 and FR.4 (including F.3)

Development
The story of the next variant of the Fairey Firefly came about when F.1 Z1835 was experimentally installed with a two-speed, two-stage supercharged Griffon 61 engine. The idea was first mooted by Fairey in early 1942, which proposed a single-seat version, a concept that the Admiralty was still not comfortable with. The Royal Navy was interested in a two-seat night fighter version, and, in October 1942, boldly gave Fairey a contract for 200 aircraft long before Z1835, by now designated as a Mk 3, was even tested.

Design
Z1835 was not an attractive looking aircraft, because the Griffon 61 needed a large 'beard-type' radiator surrounded by a large cowling in an effort to keep the powerful engine cool. Despatched to Boscombe Down for trials in July 1943, performance was found to be poor due to the lack of aerodynamics around the forward fuselage; handling was also affected. The aircraft was still 35mph faster than the F.1, but a considerably bigger increase in performance had been hoped for. Trials were abandoned, although an initial order for 100 aircraft from the Admiralty still stood.

By 1944, the idea was looked at again, and this time Firefly F.1 Z2118 was modified with leading edge radiators but retained the original aircraft's elliptical wing. By the following year, Z2118 was joined by three other prototypes, including Z1835, which were all modified to take a Griffon 72 powerplant and would effectively become the new Mk 4. The production aircraft were fitted with a Griffon 74 driving a four-blade propeller. The leading-edge radiators were installed within a pair of forward extensions at each wing root. The wingspan was reduced and had squared-off tips which increased the rate of roll. Auxiliary fuel was carried in a 55-gallon nacelle under the port wing, which was counter-balanced by a second nacelle carrying a radar scanner and equipment. These nacelles could both be used as fuel tanks, raising the aircraft's total capacity to 256 gallons. At least one aircraft, MB649, was produced as the NF.4, but, despite a healthy initial order, the contract for the type was cancelled in 1946.

Operational service
The first true prototype FR.4 flew on 25 May 1945 and was followed by a second on 21 February 1946. One of the original four prototypes, PP482, was employed to carry out operational trials with HMS *Illustrious,* and, on 25 May 1946, the first production aircraft, TW687, made its maiden flight. The FAA received its first FR.4 in July 1946, but it was not until 12 February 1947 that the FR.4 was cleared for 'restricted' shore-based operations. It was with the Royal Canadian Navy that the aircraft first entered operational service in August 1947, followed by the FAA's 810 Squadron on 1 October 1947, and then by 812 and 81 squadrons. The FR.4 only served with 810 Squadron for two years, and by the middle of 1948, 812 Squadron had converted to the FR.5, and 814 Squadron followed suit in early 1949.

Production
There were 67 FR.4s built, all by Fairey at Hayes, in the serial ranges: VG957 to VG999 and VH121 to VH144. This was from an original contract placed in June 1945 for 200 aircraft, and, from VH203 onwards, the aircraft were to have been built as NF.4s.

Technical data – Firefly FR.4	
ENGINE	One 2,100hp Rolls-Royce Griffon 74
WINGSPAN	41ft 2in; (folded) 13ft 6in
LENGTH	38ft
HEIGHT	13ft 11in
EMPTY WEIGHT	9,674lb
MAX LOADED WEIGHT	13,479lb
MAX SPEED	367mph at 14,000ft
CLIMB	5,000ft in 3mins 36secs
CEILING	31,900ft
MAX RANGE	(normal tankage) 760 miles at 209mph

Right: First delivered to RDU Cudham in October 1947, FR.4 VG985 later served with 767 and 787 squadrons before being converted to a TT.4 and joining the Indian Navy as INS-117 in September 1958. (Via Martyn Chorlton)

Below: A good view of the FR.4's redesigned frontal view, which did away with the original 'beard-type' radiator in favour of radiators buried in the leading-edge wing roots. This is Z2119, with original elliptical wings and standard tail unit, pictured on 25 May 1945. (Via Martyn Chorlton)

Firefly T.1, T.2, T.3, T.5 and T.7

Development
Owing to the large number of Fireflies in both operational and second-line service, it was only natural that a dual-controlled training variant be produced during the post-war period. Spread across five different marks, the original T.1 was a private venture by Fairey that was accepted by the FAA.

Design
The Firefly T.1, 2 and 3 were developed as pilot and observer trainers, and all were conversions of F.1s and FR.1s. All were converted at Fairey's Heaton Chapel factory and flown for the first time from Ringway. The T.1 and T.2 were designed as pilot trainers, with the instructor accommodated in the rear cockpit, where there was a second set of flying controls, instruments and a sliding canopy. The instructor's cockpit, in similar fashion to the Battle trainer, was raised so that he could see over the nose in level flight.

The first of the Firefly trainers was converted F.1, MB750 (later registered as G-AHYA), first flown from Ringway in July 1946 by Duncan Menzies. Originally known as the 'Firefly Trainer', the aircraft was extensively trialled to test whether it was suitable for deck-landing and operational training. As G-AHYA, the aircraft demonstrated across Europe and, in the hands of Group Captain R. G. Slade, took third place in the Lympne High-Speed Handicap on 31 August 1947 with an average speed of 290mph. The first of 34 production T.1s, MB473, made its maiden flight on 1 September 1947. Out of this batch, nine out of the 34 T.1s were armed with two 20mm cannons. The T.2 was an operational pilot trainer, which was fitted with a pair of 20mm cannons and gyro-gunsights, which were synchronised for both the pupil and instructor. The T.3 was a conversion of the FR.1; it made its debut in 1951 and was lacking the raised rear cockpit. This was an observer-trainer, which was unarmed but did carry the special equipment needed to train for anti-submarine operations. The T.5 was a dual-control version of 12 Royal Australian Navy (RAN) AS.5s; the work being carried out by Fairey Aviation in Australia. The final training Firefly was the T.7, which was the AS.7 converted to an observer/radar training aircraft. The T.7 only operated from shore bases, as it was not fitted with deck-arrester gear. The last T.7 was delivered to the FAA in December 1953.

Operational service
The T.1 first entered service with 736 Squadron at St Merryn in July 1948, later joining 14 other FAA squadrons before being replaced by a trainer version of the Sea Fury. The T.2 first entered service with 737 Squadron in April 1949 and the T.3 with 796 Squadron in July 1950. The T.5 entered service with 851 (RAN) Squadron in August 1954, followed by 724 (RAN) Squadron in June 1955. The T.7 served five FAA squadrons, the first being 719 Squadron in August 1953, until the aircraft was retired in December 1957 from 796 Squadron.

Production
Thirty-four T.1s were built/converted by Fairey at Heaton Chapel, as well as 57 T.2s, an unknown quantity of T.3s, 12 T.5s and approximately 140 T.7s.

Technical data – Firefly T.1	
ENGINE	One 1,735hp Rolls-Royce Griffon IIB or XII
WINGSPAN	44ft 6in; (folded) 13ft 6in
LENGTH	37ft
HEIGHT	12ft 4in
EMPTY WEIGHT	9,647lb
LOADED WEIGHT	12,485lb
MAX SPEED	305mph at 16,500ft
CLIMB	5,000ft in 2mins 42secs
CEILING	28,400ft
MAX RANGE	(normal tankage) 805 miles

Royal Australian Navy (RAN) T.5 VX375 was taken on RAN charge on 7 April 1949 to serve on board HMAS *Sydney*. Only a dozen T.5s were converted from FR.5s. (*Aeroplane*)

The prototype 'Fairey Trainer', pictured as MB750 in early 1946; by the end of the year, it was re-registered as G-AHYA. After being struck off charge from the Royal Navy in late 1948, the aircraft was sold to Thailand as SF9. (Via Martyn Chorlton)

FB.1 Gyrodyne (aka Fairey-Bennett One)

Development
Designed to take advantage of the best features of the autogyro and the helicopter, the Gyrodyne dates back to 1945. By the spring of the following year, Fairey made public its intentions to produce a new rotary-wing aircraft. The idea had been brought to the company by Dr J. A. J. Bennett, who, prior to joining Fairey in 1945, had taken over Cierva following the death of Juan de la Cierva in December 1936.

Design
Powered by a single Alvis Leonides radial engine, the attractive-looking Gyrodyne weighed in at 3,600lbs empty; half of this figure was made up of the engine and the complex transmission system. The latter comprised four units: firstly, the engine; secondly, the main gearbox with reduction gear for the propeller and main rotor drives; thirdly, an upper gearbox with double-epicyclic reduction gear; and finally, another gearbox in the starboard wing stub for reduction and pitch-changing control of the propeller.

Operational service
Fairey was awarded a contract for two prototypes under Specification E.4/46, the first of these, G-AIKF (aka VX591), was displayed as a static exhibit at the SBAC, Radlett, in September 1947. Prior to its first flight, the Gyrodyne carried out 85 hours of engine ground tests and 56 hours of rotor testing. On 7 December 1947, Gyrodyne G-AIKF, in the hands of project test pilot, Squadron Leader B. H. Arkell, made its first untethered fight from White Waltham. Flight testing continued into 1948 until March, when the aircraft was grounded and dismantled so that the transmission system could be internally checked for signs of wear and tear. In the meantime, the second prototype, registered as G-AJJP, had been completed.

On reassembly, G-AIKF was prepared for an attempt on the International Helicopter (Class G) speed record in a straight line. This record had stood, 'unofficially', since June 1938, when the Focke Achgelis Fa 61 captured it, although a Sikorsky R-5 had also 'unofficially' been recorded reaching a speed of 114.6mph. On 28 June 1948, Basil Arkell flew a pair of eastbound, and two westbound flights, along a 3km course over White Waltham. An average speed of 124.3mph was recorded, capturing the record for Britain.

A few months later, the 100km closed-circuit record was the next target. Unfortunately, only two days before the record attempt, on 17 April 1949, Gyrodyne G-AIKF crashed at Ufton, near Reading. The crash killed test pilot, F. H. Dixon, who had been Fairey's chief test pilot since 1936, and observer, Derek Garroway. Dixon had been involved in a great deal of the demonstration and development flying of the Gyrodyne, alongside Basil Arkell. The resulting investigation into the accident reported that the cause of the crash was a fatigue failure of the main rotor head. Development was brought to a halt, and the second aircraft was grounded, destined to reappear four years later as the Jet Gyrodyne.

FB.1 Gyrodyne (aka Fairey-Bennett One)

Technical data – Gyrodyne	
ENGINE	One 520hp Alvis Leonides nine-cylinder radial
ROTOR DIAMETER	51ft 9in
STUB WING-SPAN	16ft 8in
FUSELAGE LENGTH	25ft
HEIGHT	10ft 2in
EMPTY WEIGHT	3,600lb
LOADED WEIGHT	4,800lb
MAX SPEED	Approx. 140mph

Above: The prototype Gyrodyne, G-AIKF, with Squadron Leader Basil Arkell at the controls during one of many test flights out of White Waltham. (Via Martyn Chorlton)

Right: G-AJJP, the second prototype, only differed from the first aircraft in having a more passenger friendly interior and was used extensively for demonstration flying. (*Aeroplane*)

Firefly AS/FR and NF.5

Development
Very similar, externally at least, to the Firefly Mk 4, the Mk 5 represented the peak of development for the family. It also arrived in service with the FAA during a period of intensive operations, which culminated in the Korean War; a conflict in which the Firefly would serve with distinction.

Design
There were three variants of the Firefly Mk 5; the FR.5, the NF.5 and the AS.5. The latter was the anti-submarine variant, which carried detection equipment under each wing. The AS.5 was fitted with an ARI 5284 radio altimeter and an ARI 5286 sonobouy, controlled from within the observer's cockpit. The aircraft could carry up to 12 American-type sonobouys and a pair of 250lb depth charges. The night-fighter variant, the NF.5, was fitted with flame-damping manifolds and an ARI 5284 radio altimeter, this time coupled with an ARI rearward-facing radar. This simple, but effective, piece of equipment warned the pilot if an aircraft was approaching from the rear by ringing a bell in the cockpit. The FR.5 was very similar to the FR.4 but was fitted with the latest internal equipment. It was an FR.5 that finally introduced power folding wings. The first aircraft to have this luxury fitted was VX414 in January 1949. The FR.5 also had radome vibration dampers fitted to improve the radar reception.

Operational service
The first production Firefly 5, VT362, flew on 12 December 1947, and, by May 1948, the first FR.5s had joined 778 and 782 squadrons for trials, followed by the AS.5, which entered FAA service in July 1949 with 810 Squadron at St Merryn. The FR.5 was by far the most useful of the three variants (the NF.5 only served with the Dutch Navy) and later several squadrons, especially during the Korean conflict, would operate this variant rather than the later AS.6. 812 Squadron was the first operational unit to receive the FR.5 in July 1948, but it was 825 Squadron operating from HMS *Ocean* that first took the type into action over Malaya on 25 April 1952 whilst en route to Korea. 812 Squadron returned to Malaya in May 1954, its FR.5s carrying out 16 successful attacks on targets in Central Johore.

The Korean conflict saw the FR.5 extensively employed, beginning with 810 Squadron who operated from HMS *Theseus* between October 1950 and April 1951. 812 Squadron's FR.5s, now on board HMS *Glory*, took over until May 1952, when it was the turn of 825 Squadron on board HMS *Ocean*. By October 1952, 825 Squadron took on board HMS *Glory*, which remained in theatre until May 1953. It was HMS *Ocean* with 810 Squadron which saw the Armistice signed on 27 July 1953.

Technical data – Firefly AS.5	
ENGINE	One 2,245hp Rolls-Royce Griffon 74
WINGSPAN	41ft 7in
LENGTH	37ft 11in
EMPTY WEIGHT	9,674lb
LOADED WEIGHT	16,096lb
MAX SPEED	386mph at 14,000ft
CEILING	31,900ft
MAX RANGE	760 miles

Production

170 aircraft were initially ordered on 16 November 1946, but this was reduced to 117 aircraft in the serial ranges VT362 to VT381, VT392 to VT441, and VT458 to VT504. Events unfolding in the Far East prompted a second batch of 169 Firefly Mk 5s to be ordered on 20 December 1948 in the serial ranges WB243 to WB272, WB281 to WB316, WB330 to WB382, and WB391 to WB440.

Firefly AS.5 WB281, joined 810 Squadron at St Merryn on 12 August 1949. After floating over the wires on HMS *Theseus* on 8 August 1950, the aircraft crashed into WB376 and WB369, which were parked on the deck. The Firefly was struck off charge and dumped over the side the same day. (*Aeroplane*)

It took a small army of groundcrew to manually unfold the wings of a Firefly prior to the arrival of power-folding wings from VX414 onwards. This is FR.5 VT413, which was later converted to a U.9. Its fate was sealed when a Sea Vixen shot the drone down off Malta on 23 November 1961. (*Aeroplane*)

Firefly AS.6

Design

To improve the Firefly's anti-submarine capability, a sacrifice had to be made, and, in the case of the Firefly AS.6, the defensive 20mm cannons were removed. To compromise, the AS.6 had hard points fitted to the underside of the wings, able to carry 16 3in RPs, carried in a group of eight in two rows of four under each wing. These hard points could also carry depth charges, mines or sonobouys. The first production Firefly AS.6, WB505, made its maiden flight on 23 March 1949 and was delivered to the FAA on 26 May 1950.

Operational service

The first unit to receive the Firefly AS.6 was the Royal Australian Navy's 817 Squadron, under the command of Lieutenant Commander R. B. Lunberg, RN. After reforming at St Merryn with AS.5s, the unit, as part of the 21st CAG, set sail on board HMS *Sydney* for Australia. When the unit arrived at Nowra on 6 December 1950, it also took charge of several AS.6s. For the FAA, it was 814 Squadron, which had reformed at Culdrose on 22 November 1950, under the command of Lieutenant Commander A. C. Lindsay DFC, RN, that first received the AS.6 in January 1951. Along with 809 Squadron (operating the Sea Hornet NF.21), the unit formed the 7th NAG (Night Air Group), the first all-weather group. After embarking on HMS *Vengeance* to work-up for its part in the 7th NAG during May 1951, the unit managed to carry out 927 hours of night training, for which it received the annual Boyd Trophy for its efforts.

The AS.6 served with 13 squadrons in the anti-submarine role, the majority of its work being carried out over the North Sea and Mediterranean, keeping tabs on Soviet movements. By 1955, the AS.6 was being withdrawn from FAA service, making way for the Gannet, but the Royal Australian Navy continued to operate the type until 1958. One of the Royal Australian Navy units, 816 Squadron, used its AS.6s to take part in atomic bomb testing on the Monte Bello Islands in October 1952. The last bastion for the AS.6 was 851 (RAN) Squadron, which was reformed at Nowra on 3 August 1954, specifically to carry out anti-submarine training. The unit was disbanded on 13 January 1958, taking the AS.6 with it. The AS.6 also served extensively in many second-line FAA squadrons, including 703, 703A, 719, 723, 724, 737, 737X, 744, 751, 767, 771, 782 and 796 squadrons.

Technical data – Firefly AS.6	
ENGINE	One 2,245hp Rolls-Royce Griffon 74
WINGSPAN	41ft 7in
LENGTH	37ft 11in
HEIGHT	13ft 11in
EMPTY WEIGHT	9,674lb
LOADED WEIGHT	16,096lb
MAX SPEED	386mph at 14,000ft
CEILING	31,900ft
MAX RANGE	760 miles

Production

The first production batch, for just 14 aircraft, WB505 to WB510 and WB516 to WB553, was ordered in February 1949, although these serials were preceded by WB422 to WB440 (16), which were AS.5s converted to AS.6 standard. A total of 133 'new-build' AS.6s were constructed between January 1947 and September 1951.

First flown on 15 September 1951, Firefly AS.6 WJ121 is pictured before the aircraft was delivered to 814 Squadron at Culdrose. The Firefly later served with RAN from early 1953. (*Aeroplane*)

Firefly AS.6 WH632, aka '211/FD' of 1840 Squadron, based at Hal Far. The Malta-based unit flew the AS.6 from July 1951 to May 1956. (*Aeroplane*)

Firefly TT.1, 4, 5 and 6

Development
Fairey did not miss a trick when it came to broadening the appeal of the Fairey Firefly during the post-war period. This even included presenting the aircraft as a potential target-tug, a role that it was particularly well suited to.

Design
The first of four different marks of Firefly target tug was the TT.1, which actually came about from a proposal from Svensk Flygjänst, which had won a contract to support Swedish anti-aircraft units. Modifications for this latest mark included the fitment of a windmill-operated (windlass arm) RFD Type 'B' and a Mk 2B cable winch, mounted on the port side of the fuselage between the pilot's and cable operator's positions. Next was the TT.4, based on the Firefly 4, which was fitted with an air-driven Mk Type G winch mounted under the centreline of the fuselage, directly below the wing. The bomb-shaped pod made it much easier to convert any Firefly 4, 5 or 6 into a target-tug without major modifications. Two TT.5s were created for the Royal Australian Navy from a conversion kit supplied by Fairey, and four Royal Australian Navy AS.6s were converted into TT.5s in the same way.

Operational service
Out of the 14 TT.1s built, Svensk Flygjänst ordered 12 of them, the first of which arrived in early 1949. The Swedish company later ordered four more TT.1s, which remained in service until late 1963. Denmark also ordered a pair of TT.1s and later converted four ex-Royal Canadian Navy Mk 1s as well. The Indian Navy is also believed to have operated at least four TT.1s. The most successful of the TT family was the TT.4, the first of which entered service with 771 Squadron at Lee-on-Solent in November 1951. When 771 Squadron retired the type in August 1955, it was transferred to the strength of 700 Squadron, which had just reformed at Ford. The squadron continued to fly the TT.4 until February 1957, when target towing duties were placed in civilian hands with Airwork FRU. The FRU operated the TT.4 until December 1958. The TT.4 also served with the Indian Navy from 1955 to 1958.

The two TT.5s first entered service with 723 (RAN) Squadron in November 1954 until October 1956. 851 (RAN) Squadron is also credited with operating at least one of the TT.5s, while 725 (RAN) Squadron is 'officially' recorded as using the type from January 1958 to May 1959. One of these was WB271, which returned to the UK to serve with Royal Navy Historic Flight. All four TT.6s were also operated in Australia

Technical data – Firefly TT.1	
ENGINE	One 1,730hp Rolls-Royce Griffon IIB
WINGSPAN	44ft 6in
LENGTH	37ft 7in
HEIGHT	12ft 4in
LOADED WEIGHT	14,020lb
MAX SPEED	316mph at 14,000ft
MAX RANGE	1,300 miles

by the Royal Australian Navy, initially with 725 (RAN) Squadron at Nowra from January 1958 to May 1959 and finally with 724 (RAN) Squadron from November 1962 to March 1966, also based at Nowra.

Production

Fourteen Firefly TT.1s were initially ordered, 12 of them for Sweden and two for Denmark. Later, Sweden ordered four additional aircraft, while five were delivered to the Indian Navy. Twenty-eight TT.4s were ordered/converted, including five for the Indian Navy. VX388 and WB271 were converted to TT.5s, and WB518, WD826, WD828 and WJ109 were converted to TT.6 standard.

The Indian Navy ordered ten Firefly TTs, five TT.1s and five TT.4s between 1955 and 1958. INS112, a TT.1, is pictured on a pre-delivery test flight over England. Today, the aircraft is the only survivor of the ten TTs and is on display at the Naval Aviation Museum in Goa. (*Aeroplane*)

Originally delivered to RDU Culham in 1947 as an FR.4, VH127 was converted to a TT.4 in 1952. Ten years later, the aircraft was retained for 'historical purposes', first arriving at the FAA Museum, Yeovilton, in 1972. Placed in storage at Wroughton in 1988, VH127 returned to Yeovilton four years later and today is on display in Hall 1. (*Aeroplane*)

Gannet (aka the Fairey 'Q', GR.17 and Fairey 17)

Development
As the range and capability of enemy submarines increased during the latter stages of World War Two, the necessity to develop an anti-submarine aircraft increased in priority. The Swordfish found itself carrying out this vital role from fleet and smaller aircraft carriers, but it was obvious that a newer, more dedicated machine was needed. The remit was covered in Specification GR.17/45, which called for a two-seat carrier-borne aircraft fitted with a powerful search radar. This radar was to be capable of detecting very small targets, such as a snorkel or a conning tower, at long range. As well as finding the submarine, the aircraft would also have to have the capability of destroying it, either on the surface or submerged with a variety of weapons, including an airborne homing torpedo.

Design
Designs for GR.17/45 were presented by Blackburn, Fairey and Short, and two prototypes from each company were ordered. H. E. Chaplin led the Fairey design team, which initially designed its latest aircraft around the Rolls-Royce Tweed double-propeller-turbine engine. The Tweed was dropped in 1947 in favour of a pair of Armstrong Siddeley Mamba turbines, which were coupled together. The prototype was fitted with a 2,950ehp Double Mamba A.S.M.D.1 which drove a pair of co-axial, counter-rotating propellers through a single gearbox, which had a clutch gear that enabled the pilot to shut one engine down. By doing this, the range could be dramatically extended while the aircraft had the inbuilt safety and load-carrying ability of two engines but remained small enough to operate from an aircraft carrier. Initially known as the Fairey 'Q' or '17', the aircraft had a large weapons bay, which was later made even bigger to accommodate a pair of homing torpedoes. The first two prototypes were designed as two-seaters, and it was not until the arrival of the third, that the aircraft, which would become known as the Gannet, was fitted with a third crew position at the rear.

Operational service
The first prototype, VR546, was first flown by Group Captain R. G. Slade from Aldermaston on 19 September 1949. The flight testing phase that followed was not an easy one for the Gannet, which was hampered by a host of handling problems caused by the wide flight envelope demanded. The problem was not the layout of the engines but the way the power was delivered through a large range of settings, and this was further complicated by various flight conditions when the aircraft's Fairey-Youngman flaps were employed. By the time that the third prototype, WE488, was ordered in July 1949, the majority of the handling problems had been illuminated. However, further trials would be needed, as the aircraft now had a third cockpit and a larger weapons bay. Trials on board HMS *Illustrious* and *Albion* in 1951 exposed further problems, but by then, a super-priority order had been placed for 100 production aircraft.

Production
Two Gannet prototypes, VR546 and VR557, were ordered on 12 August 1946 to Contract 6/Acft/494/CB.9(b) to Specification GR.17/45. One Gannet prototype, WE488, was ordered on 19 July 1949 to contract 6/Acft/3546 and the same specification.

Gannet (aka the Fairey 'Q', GR.17 and Fairey 17)

Technical data – Gannet AS.1	
ENGINE	One Armstrong Siddeley Double Mamba (A.S.M.D.1)
WINGSPAN	54ft 4in
LENGTH	43ft
HEIGHT	13ft 8½in
EMPTY WEIGHT	15,069lb
LOADED WEIGHT	19,600lb
MAX SPEED	310mph

The prototype Gannet, VR546, was built at Hayes and transported by road to Aldermaston, from where Group Captain R. G. Slade flew the aircraft on its maiden flight on 19 September 1949. (*Aeroplane*)

Ordered in July 1949 to a separate contract, WE488 was a three-seater prototype, although the rear cockpit was a mock-up at this stage. The aircraft first flew from White Waltham on 10 May 1951. (Via Martyn Chorlton)

Firefly AS.7 and T.7

Development

The Firefly AS.7 came about because of an urgent need for an anti-submarine aircraft pending the arrival of the Gannet. However, the AS.7 was never designed to actually destroy the offending submarine, merely to find it. In the end, the anti-submarine role was temporarily and effectively filled by the Avenger AS.4.

Design

The AS.7 differed in many areas from the AS.6, but its general appearance resembled the Firefly F.1 because of the installation of the water/methanol-injected Griffon 57 (and later Griffon 59) engine, which needed the 'beard-type' radiator. The latter removed the need for the leading-edge radiators, which had been introduced by the FR.4. The rear observer's cockpit was another key difference; it was increased in size to accommodate a pair of radar operators under a large, bulbous canopy. A powerful ASV Mk 19A radar set was also installed; its scanner being accommodated in a radome under the starboard wing, while a similar nacelle was used as an auxiliary fuel tank under the port wing. The AS.7 retained the original F.1 full-span wings but was also fitted with an increased area fin and rudder. As mentioned, it had not been planned for the aircraft to have any striking power once in service, but it did have the capability to carry a wide range of stores under the wings. It was not fitted with any defensive armament.

Technical data – Firefly AS.7	
ENGINE	One 1,925hp Rolls-Royce Griffon 59
WINGSPAN	44ft 6in
LENGTH	38ft 3in
HEIGHT	13ft 3in
WING AREA	342 sq ft
EMPTY WEIGHT	11,016lb
LOADED WEIGHT	13,970lb
MAX SPEED	300mph at 10,750ft
CRUISING SPEED	257mph
INITIAL CLIMB	1,500ft/min
CEILING	25,500ft
MAX RANGE	860 miles at 166mph

Delivered to Handling Squadron, RAF Manby, on 2 October 1952, AS.7 WJ154 was transferred to RDU Anthorn in May 1953, then AHU Lossiemouth in October 1956, only to be retired in August 1958 with just 27.20 flying hours on the clock. (Via Martyn Chorlton)

Photographs of AS.7s actually flying for an FAA unit are rare. This pair are from 719 Squadron based at Eglinton, Northern Ireland. Nearest to the camera is WK368, which only served the unit from March 1953 to September 1954 following a taxiing accident. (Via Martyn Chorlton)

F.D.1 (E.10/47, Type R or the Fairey Delta One)

Development
With its long history of producing naval aircraft behind it, Fairey had been considering the design of a delta-wing fighter that could be vertically launched from warships for quite some time. Specification E.10/47 followed, calling for a delta-winged research aircraft that could test the theories that Fairey had already researched. The company's response was the Fairey Delta One (F.D.1), originally referred to as the 'Fairey Type R'. Prior to the construction of the full-sized machine, a large number of models with a span of 10ft were built and at first launched from Aberporth. However, following of couple of potentially dangerous incidents involving the use of hydrogen peroxide and methanol hydrazine, which, if mixed, were highly explosive, test launches were continued from the tank-landing craft HMS *Sulva* out in Cardigan Bay.

These small but potent models were powered by a single Fairey-built Beta 1 bi-fuel engine with twin combustion chambers capable of producing up to 1,800lbs of thrust. Thrust for the first stage of the launch was provided by a pair of 600lb rockets. The first Fairey model was launched from HMS *Sulva* on 1 May 1949, but this situation was not ideal, and the remainder of the trials were transferred to the Long-Range Weapons Establishment at Woomera in Australia.

Design
The full-size F.D.1 was still not a larger aircraft, its span only being 19ft 6ins. Powered by a single Derwent engine, the aircraft also had the provision to be fitted with a pair of booster rockets, as per the models, but these were never installed.

The F.D.1 was a 'tubby' looking mid-wing delta, with a large intake in the nose for the engine to breathe. The aircraft was fitted with a tricycle undercarriage, despite being originally designed with a jettisonable one (the aircraft landing on a skid), which cleverly concealed itself within the circular fuselage through the main gear retracting outwards and then rearwards through 45 degrees. Control, both fore-and-aft and lateral was by powered elevons fitted to the trailing edge of the wing. A big powerful rudder was also fitted, and, as well as conventional brakes, a drogue chute was fitted for landing. If the aircraft got into trouble in flight, a pair of spin-recovery chutes were fitted into the wing tips.

Operational service
The first of three F.D.1s ordered, VX350, was flown for the first time by Gordon Slade from Boscombe Down for just 17 minutes on 12 March 1951. Prior to this, taxiing trials had been carried out at Ringway from May 1950 by Peter Swiss and Slade. By this time, the Air Ministry had lost interest in the potential of a vertical take-off fighter, and even before VX350 had flown, a second F.D.1, VX364, had been cancelled. The third aircraft, VX357, was cancelled in May 1953, and like the VX364 had reached an advanced stage of construction. Both were scrapped at Fairey's Stockport factory. VX350 continued to be used for trials flying and provided Fairey with a huge amount of useful data, which proved very useful for the F.D.2, despite the latter having very little in common from an appearance point of view. VX350 was unfortunately written off on 6 February 1956 when it swung on landing, seriously damaging the undercarriage at Boscombe Down. The aircraft was then despatched to P&EE Foulness in October 1956, where it was later scrapped.

F.D.1 (E.10/47, Type R or the Fairey Delta One)

Technical Data – F.D.1	
ENGINE	One 3,600lb Rolls-Royce Derwent 8 turbojet
WINGSPAN	19ft 6½in
LENGTH	26ft 3in
LOADED WEIGHT	6,800lb
MAX SPEED	628mph at 10,000ft
INITIAL RATE OF CLIMB	9,300 ft/min
CLIMB	15,000ft in 1min 54secs

Right: The one and only Fairey F.D.1, VX350 (c/n F.8466), during an early test flight, showing the air brakes at the inner trailing edge of the wing in the extended position. (*Aeroplane*)

Below: Streaming its drogue parachute, F.D.1 VX350 slows after landing at the 1954 SBAC display at Farnborough. (*Aeroplane*)

Firefly U.8 and U.9

Development
The story of the Firefly drones began in the late 1940s at Hayes and White Waltham, where development had been progressing well. This work was transferred to the Stockport factory in 1952. The idea was to produce an aircraft that could be used to support guided-missile testing, which was being carried out in Britain and at Woomera in Australia. A further requirement was that the aircraft had to be capable of being operated by a normal crew or by a remote-control system controlled from the ground.

Design
The first of the two drones was designated as the Firefly U.8, which used the T.7 airframe. A Mk 8 autopilot was fitted, which had already been successfully tested by the RAE in an Avro Lancaster. The autopilot was monitored from the ground, and all flying adjustments were controlled by radio. The throttle, flaps, propeller and undercarriage were controlled by actuators. The arrester hook was not originally fitted to the T.7, but it proved a useful piece of equipment, especially when a drone returned to base under remote control. Only the most basic of flying instruments and controls were left in place for a 'real' crew. A pair of nacelles were attached to each wing tip, containing four cine cameras in each, for recording the effects of a missile strike or near miss. By 1955, the supply of U.8 drones was running low, because of successful missile strikes and various flying accidents. The MoS placed an order for 40 additional drones, and, to accommodate this, Fairey offered to convert surplus FR.5s. These were designated as Firefly U.9s, which used the same autopilot as the U.8. Conversion work began in 1956.

Operational service
The first U.8 made its maiden flight from Ringway on 30 December 1954. The majority of U.8s served the RAE from Llanbedr, and it was from there that the first operational flight took place in February 1955. Flying the U.8 was a complex and expensive operation, which involved a second Firefly flying as a 'shepherd' with its own remote-control equipment and two further sets of equipment on the ground to take over when landing the drone. On 29 September 1955, the first U.8 was shot down by a de Havilland Venom launching a Firestreak missile. U.8s also played a key role in the development of the Armstrong Siddeley Seaslug surface-to-air missile, and several more were claimed by the fledgling Sidewinder.

The first U.9 took to the air on 13 December 1956, and, by January 1958, had entered service with 728B Squadron, based at Stretton, alongside a few remaining U.8s. On 1 March 1958, the unit relocated to Hal Far, from where the first remote control flight was carried out on 8 July. Like the U.8 before it, the U.9 played an active role in the development of the Seaslug, which was being fired from RFA Girdle Ness. By 1959, the

Technical data – Firefly U.8 and U.9	
ENGINE	(U.8) One 1,925hp Rolls-Royce Griffon 59; (U.9) One 2,100hp Griffon 74
WINGSPAN	(U.8) 44ft 6in; (U.9) 41ft 2in
LENGTH	(U.8) 38ft 3in; (U.9) 38ft
HEIGHT	(U.8) 13ft 3in; (U.9) 13ft 11in
EMPTY WEIGHT	(U.8) 11,016lb; (U.9) 9,674lb
MAX LOADED WEIGHT	(U.8) 13,970lb; (U.9) 13,479lb

Fireflies were supplemented by Meteor drones and finally by Canberras in May 1961. U.9s were also used by 728B Squadron for Firestreak testing in later 1958, all of which were fired by Sea Venoms of 893 Squadron from HMS *Victorious*. By late 1961, the final few U.9s were being despatched by anti-aircraft guns from Royal Navy warships; the last being shot down on 29 November 1961 by the guns of HMS *Duchess*.

Built from new as a U.8, WM856 first flew on 2 February 1954. It was delivered to RAE Llanbedr in November 1956 but was lost in March 1958 when the drone crashed into the sea, the crash was presumed to have been caused by a lack of fuel. (Via Martyn Chorlton)

The very first U.8 completed at Stockport was WM810, which first flew from Ringway on 27 November 1953. Despite crashing into the sea off Aberporth in September 1957, the drone was repaired, only to become a total loss while operating from Llanbedr in November 1959. (Via Martyn Chorlton)

Gannet AS.1

Development
Within two years of the priority production order for 100 Gannets being placed, the first production aircraft were already in the air, but it was still more than year before the type reached frontline service. To fill the Royal Navy's capability gap, 100 Grumman Avenger AS.4s were ordered through the Mutual Defence Aid Programme, the first entering FAA service in May 1953, and many were still in frontline service up to 1955, eventually being replaced by the Gannet.

Design
Compared to the prototypes, the Gannet AS.1 was powered by a Double Mamba 100 engine. It had its main undercarriage repositioned and its nose wheel revised. The connection between the flaps and the tailplane incidence gear was also improved, so that the aircraft's trim was automatically adjusted as the flaps were raised and lowered. The first production Gannet AS.1, WN339, was first flown by Peter Twiss from Northolt on 9 June 1953. WN339 was later flown to White Waltham for test work and the installation of operational equipment. The third production aircraft, WN341, was used for carrier trials on HMS *Illustrious* and *Eagle* during October 1953, which included night flying.

Operational service
The Gannet first entered FAA service on 5 April 1954, when four aircraft, WN347 to WN350, were handed over to 703X Flight (part of 703 Squadron Service Trials Unit) under the command of Lieutenant Commander F. E. Cowtan at Ford. The first operational unit to receive the Gannet AS.1 was 826 Squadron at Lee-on-Solent under the command of Lieutenant Commander G. F. Birch in January 1955. By early June, the unit's eight Gannet AS.1s had embarked aboard the recently updated HMS *Eagle* for a cruise of the Mediterranean. Fifteen AS.1s also joined the Royal Australian Navy, serving with 816 and 817 squadrons on board HMAS *Melbourne* and *Sydney*, respectively. Eventually, nine operational and one reserve FAA squadron were re-equipped with the Gannet AS.1, which served until the late 1960s with the Royal Australian Navy but was quickly superseded by the AS.4 with frontline FAA units during the mid to late 1950s. The following units also operated the Gannet AS.1; 700, 703, 719, 724, 725, 737, 744, 796, 812, 815, 820, 824, 825, 831, 847 and 1840 squadrons.

Technical data – Gannet AS.1	
ENGINE	One 2,950ehp Double Mamba 100 coupled-turboprop driving co-axial counter-rotating four blade propellers; WN340 was fitted with a Double Mamba Mk 3 engine
WINGSPAN	54ft 4in
LENGTH	43ft
HEIGHT	13ft 8½in
EMPTY WEIGHT	15,069lb
LOADED WEIGHT	19,600lb
MAX SPEED	310mph

Production

In total, 180 Gannet AS.1s were built, 116 of them at Hayes and 64 at Stockport, within the serial ranges WN339 to WN464, XA319 to XA436, XG784 to XG826, and XG898.

The tenth production Gannet AS.1, WN348, was delivered to AHU Ford on 15 March 1954 and on to 703X Flight, also at Ford on 5 April. During deck trials from HMS *Albion* on 25 August 1954, the aircraft stalled on take-off and ditched near the starboard bow. The pilot was rescued, but Mr J. D. Byrne of the RAE was killed. (Via Martyn Chorlton)

The RAN ordered 36 Gannet AS.1s, including XA326, which served with 817 Squadron aboard HMAS *Melbourne* from August 1955 and then completed two tours of duty with 816 Squadron. (Via Martyn Chorlton)

Jet Gyrodyne

Development
By late 1953, the second Gyrodyne prototype re-emerged in a completely different guise. Behind the scenes, a large amount of testing had been carried out at White Waltham on static rigs to prove the principles of a tip-jet rotor-driven system. A contract was already in place from the MoS to carry out further research into the system, and it was time to test the idea on a live aircraft. This was essential, not only to continue development and testing of the tip-jet, but also to test the aircraft's handling and to begin the lengthy process of creating the procedures for the operation of a convertible or compound helicopter. Named the Jet Gyrodyne in early 1954 and serialled XD759 (a duplicated serial shared with a Canadair Sabre F.4), later changed to XJ389, the aircraft made its first tethered flight at White Waltham with John N. Dennis at the controls. By late January 1954, the aircraft made a 'free' flight for the first time.

Design
Only the fuselage, stub wings, tail unit and tricycle undercarriage of the original Gyrodyne were retained. The Leonides engine drove a pair of variable-pitch pusher propellers via gearbox and shafts in the stub-wings. The propellers gave propulsion in the cruise and at lower speeds, and directional control was achieved via the rudder pedals, thanks to a differential pitch-change placed on top of the collective-pitch action. This is where the similarity to the original Gyrodyne comes to an end, with a third drive direct from the gearbox to a pair of Rolls-Royce Merlin centrifugal compressors mounted together under the main rotor pylon. These compressors provided air to the tip burners at the ends of the two-blade rotor.

While the theory seemed easy to convey, in practice, flying the aircraft was very difficult, aggravated by the fact that the Jet Gyrodyne weighed in at a hefty 2,720kg. This meant that the Leonides engine had to be operated at full boost, and, even then, the aircraft could only momentarily maintain level flight. It was not until 1 March 1955 that John Dennis managed to carry out a successful transition from a vertical take-off to a level flight cruise; the first such exercise in any aircraft.

Operational service
From that first transition in March 1955 through to September 1956, the Jet Gyrodyne carried out 190 transitions and 140 auto-rotative landings. By then, the techniques needed to carry out an in-flight

Technical data – Jet Gyrodyne	
ENGINE	One Alvis Leonides nine-cylinder radial engine and two wing tip compress air/fuel burning jet engines
ROTOR DIAMETER	51ft 9in
FUSELAGE LENGTH	25ft
HEIGHT	10ft 2in
EMPTY WEIGHT	3,600lb
GROSS WEIGHT	6,000lb
MAX SPEED	140mph

tip burner relight were now understood and could be carried out with relative ease. While this stage had taken 18 months of hard work by highly experienced test pilots, once the correct procedures were in place the reward came when six MoS pilots were taught how to fly the Jet Gyrodyne after only one hour of instruction. The aircraft paved the way for the Rotodyne, and, when ground testing of its bigger younger sibling began, the Jet Gyrodyne was retired. Earmarked for the scrap man in 1961, the Jet Gyrodyne was saved and today resides in the Museum of Berkshire Aviation.

Right: Displaying its original military serial, XD759, the Jet Gyrodyne, with John Dennis at the controls, makes an early untethered flight at White Waltham in 1954. (Via Martyn Chorlton)

Below: With its twin engine-driven propellers in the pusher configuration and jet-driven rotor, the Jet Gyrodyne was an advancement of the basic Gyrodyne theory. (*Aeroplane*)

Gannet T.2

Design
The prototype Gannet T.2, WN365, was allotted for conversion on 12 March 1954 from an AS.1 on the production line at Hayes. After the work had been carried out, the aircraft was transported to White Waltham by road on 8 June 1954 and was first flown on 16 August. Fitted with dual controls in the front two cockpits, the instructor in the rear had access to a periscope, which retracted when the forward canopy was opened. The radar and its supporting equipment were removed, while the spare rear cockpit could be used by a radio operator or to carry a pair of passengers.

Operational service
The first of 36 production aircraft, XA508, joined 737 Squadron at Eglinton under the command of Lietenant Commander D. W. Pennick in February 1955 and remained on strength until the unit disbanded in November 1957. The Gannet T.2 also served the following FAA units; 700, 719, 725, 728, 796, 812, 820, 824, 825 and 1840 squadrons. The majority of these units had given up the type by the late 1950s, only 725 Squadron kept the T.2 into the next decade, retiring its aircraft in May 1961. The Gannet T.2 also served the Royal Australian Navy. Three aircraft remained on strength until the late 1960s with 724 and 816 squadrons. Two T.2s, ex-XA521 and ex-XG574, were refurbished by Fairey for service with the Indonesian Navy as LA-18 and LA-17, respectively. While some minor incidents did occur during the T.2's decade of service, not one aircraft was destroyed in a flying accident, which is quite remarkable for a trainer.

Production
In total, 37 Gannet T.2s were built at Hayes and flown from White Waltham. The prototype, WN365, a converted AS.1, and two production batches of 23 and 13 aircraft, respectively, were built. The first batch, XA508 to XA531 (c/n F.9328 to F.9350) was ordered to Contract 6/Acft/8203/CB.9(a) on 7 May 1952, and the second, XG869 to XG881 (c/n F.9398 to F.9410), ordered to Contract 6/Acft/10545/CB.9(A), on 25 June 1954.

Converted from the AS.1 production to become the prototype T.2, WN365 was delivered to Fairey at White Waltham on 8 June 1954, before making its first flight from Northolt on 16 August 1954. (*Aeroplane*)

Gannet T.2

Technical data – Gannet T.2	
ENGINE	One 2,950ehp Double Mamba 100 (A.S.M.D.1)
WINGSPAN	54ft 4in
LENGTH	43ft
HEIGHT	13ft 8½in
EMPTY WEIGHT	15,069lb
LOADED WEIGHT	19,600lb
MAX SPEED	310mph

The prototype Gannet T.2, WN365, being demonstrated at the SBAC show at Farnborough in September 1954, only days after its maiden flight. (Via Martyn Chorlton)

The third production T.2, XA510 was from the first batch of 24 aircraft, which were built at Hayes and first flown from White Waltham. First flown on 1 January 1955, XA510 was retired in 1968 having flown only 356.45 flying hours. (Via Martyn Chorlton)

F.D.2

Development

During the post-war period, Britain was lacking with regard to supersonic aircraft design. However, the MoS attempted to rectify this by issuing Specification ER.103, which called for an experimental aircraft that could reach Mach 1.5 at 36,000ft; English Electric proposed its P.1 and Fairey its Delta Two. While P.1 evolved into the successful Lightning, the F.D.2 would be used to investigate aircraft performance at both transonic and supersonic speeds.

Design

A contract for a pair of aircraft was placed in October 1950, but, because all focus was on Gannet production at the time, design work on the F.D.2 did not begin until mid-1952. Designed with a wing that had the lowest thickness-to-chord ratio that had ever been attempted before, the F.D.2, like its predecessor, was of a delta-wing arrangement, and that is where all similarities end. The aircraft's very narrow fuselage was designed around the Avon powerplant and the outer skin of the F.D.1 was never any more than 5in from the exterior of the engine. One of the many novel features of this outstanding aircraft was that the entire nose, cockpit and all, could be dropped through 10 degrees to give the pilot a better field of view when the aircraft was being flown at a high angle of attack. This same system was later adopted for Concorde.

Operational service

The first aircraft, WG774, took to the air in the hands of Peter Twiss from Boscombe Down on 6 October 1954. Twiss rapidly gained confidence in flying the F.D.2, which he described, very early on, as having great promise. By 17 November, Twiss was carrying out the aircraft's 14th flight, when, at 30,000ft and approaching Mach 0.9, the Avon engine became starved of fuel because of a system fault. Despite being 30 miles from Boscombe Down, Twiss managed to get WG774 back to the airfield, although some damage was caused in the subsequent crash landing, which eventually delayed the flight programme for eight months.

Technical data – F.D.2	
ENGINE	One 10,000lb Rolls-Royce Avon 200
WINGSPAN	26ft 10in
LENGTH	51ft 7½in
HEIGHT	11ft
WING AREA	360 sq ft
EQUIPPED EMPTY WEIGHT	11,000lb
MAX TAKE-OFF WEIGHT	13,884lb
MAX SPEED	(low) 748mph; (above 36,000ft) Mach 1.7 (1,222mph)
INITIAL CLIMB	(without after-burner) 4,750 ft/min; (with after-burner) 15,000 ft/min
TIME TO 40,000ft	Climbing at Mach 0.93, 2.5 min
MAX RANGE	(without after-burner) 830 miles

Fitted with a new wing and various other modifications, the F.D.2 was back in the air again in March 1955 and by October, had finally gone supersonic. These early flights beyond the sound barrier were actually achieved without the use of re-heat (still in its infancy) or maximum throttle. By the following month, the F.D.2 was recording speeds of Mach 1.56 (1,028mph) at 36,000ft and beyond with ease, so it was decided that the aircraft should make an attempt on the world speed record. On 10 March 1956, Peter Twiss flew WG774 along a course 9.7 miles in length between Chichester and RNAS Ford. Flying at 38,000ft, eight pairs of runs were flown recording an average speed of 1,132mph, which was 310mph faster than the previous record. This outstanding achievement stood until 12 December 1957, when an F-101A Voodoo recorded a speed of 1,208mph.

The second aircraft, WG777, was first flown, again by Twiss from Boscombe, on 15 February 1956, but by this time the Air Ministry was losing interest in the development of high-speed fighters. Both aircraft went on to carry out valuable flight testing, especially WG774, which later became the BAC 221 and played a crucial role in the development of Concorde. Both machines survive today, WG774 at the FAA Museum in Ilchester and WG777 at the RAF Museum at Cosford.

Right: **The Fairey F.D.2, WG774, was the fastest aircraft in the world from 10 March 1956 to 12 December 1957.** (*Aeroplane*)

Below: **The Fairey F.D.2, WG774, pictured en route to the 1956 SBAC air show at Farnborough.** (*Aeroplane*)

Ultra-light Helicopter

Development
In 1953, the War Office, in collaboration with the Air Ministry and the MoS, began compiling a specification for a straightforward, inexpensive helicopter that the Army could use for reconnaissance, casualty evacuation and training duties. The criteria were demanding, and included the ability to be part-dismantled and be transported on a three-ton truck. Six manufacturers responded to the original specification, H.144T, which was won by Fairey in July 1954. Named the Ultra-light, Fairey incorporated the same rotor-tip drive system that it had already developed for its Jet Gyrodyne and the forthcoming Rotodyne.

Design
Power for the small helicopter was provided by a Palouste BnPe.2 engine, which was being built under licence by Blackburn and General Aircraft. Thrust was diverted to the tip-jets via an oversized centrifugal compressor. The compressed air travelled through a lagged duct to the rotor head and, combined with fuel, continued on to the tip-jets. The prototype used a direct tilting-head control, but this was later replaced by a hydraulically powered system for the cyclic-pitch, which was also fitted to later Ultra-lights. Flying controls were the same as any other helicopter, the collective-pitch lever carried a twist-grip throttle for raising the engine rpm, which simultaneously increased the air pressure to the tip jets. A normal stick was used for roll and pitch, and rudder pedals were used for directional control via a steel-skinned rudder.

Operational service
The prototype, XJ924, made its maiden flight from White Waltham in the hands of W. R. Gellatly on 14 August 1955, a mere 13 months since design work had begun. Unfortunately, by mid-1956, the MoS had lost interest (for economic reasons), but Fairey continued to develop it as a private venture. During 1957, the Piasecki Aircraft Corporation in the USA showed a great deal of interest in what Fairey was achieving, which, in turn, led to the US Army evaluating the Ultra-light, although nothing

Technical data – Ultra-light Helicopter	
ENGINE	One Turboméca Palouste BnPe.2 turbojet
ROTOR DIAMETER	28ft 3½in
FUSELAGE LENGTH	15ft
HEIGHT	8ft 2in
LOADED WEIGHT	1,800lb
VERTICAL RATE OF CLIMB	950 ft/min
MAX RATE OF CLIMB	1,350 ft/min at sea level
HOVERING CEILING	4,800ft
CRUISING SPEED	95mph
MAX RANGE	180 miles
MAX ENDURANCE	2hrs 30 mins

came of it. The second Ultra-light, XJ928, was used by Fairey as a development aircraft with a different cabin which, among other things, was modified to carry a single stretcher. XJ928 was later registered as G-AOUJ and fitted with hydraulic controls. The prototype, XJ924, had already appeared at the SBAC in 1955, but it was the turn of XJ936 for the 1956 event, where it performed as the main demonstration aircraft. Later aircraft were trialled by the RAE at Bedford, the College of Aeronautics at Cranfield and the Royal Navy. The latter saw G-AOUJ performing trials with HMS *Grenville* in late 1957. The small helicopter successfully carried out 70 landings and take-offs in winds of up to 62kts, during which time the deck pitched up to 3.66m and rolled through 14 degrees. Frustratingly for Fairey, the entire project was reluctantly abandoned in 1959.

Production

Six Ultra-lights were built; the prototype, XJ924, followed by XJ928 (G-AOUJ). XJ930 was delivered direct to the MoS and XJ936 (later G-AOUK) first flew on 24 August 1956. The fifth aircraft was G-APJJ, which was evaluated by the Royal Navy in 1958, and the sixth airframe never flew.

Test pilot W. R. Gellatly (facing the camera), stands behind the prototype Fairey Ultra-light, XJ924, at the 1955 SBAC airshow at Farnborough. (Via Martyn Chorlton)

Gannet T.5

Design
Like the Gannet AS.4 from which it evolved, the second trainer version of the big anti-submarine aircraft, the T.5, came about because the rising weight of the AS.1, which resulted in the need for a more powerful engine. Basically, the T.5s were converted from the final eight T.2s on the Hayes production line by fitting a 3,035ehp Double Mamba 101 engine. Only nine were built, and the first production aircraft, XG882, flew for the first time from Northolt on 1 March 1957.

Operational service
The Gannet T.5 officially entered service with 849 HQ Squadron at Culdrose in September 1961, although one aircraft, XG887, was briefly on the strength of 719 Squadron at Eglinton in February/March 1959. The T.5 also served with the Station Flight at Culdrose before transferring to 849 Squadron and Station Flight/MTPS at Abbotsinch, NARIU Lee-on-Solent and NASU Brawdy and Lossiemouth. The T.5 remained in service with 849 Squadron until January 1976. Only one aircraft was lost in service, on 1 July 1963, when XG887, being flown by H. Proudlove of the Ferry Flight, Rochester, was returning from Short Brothers, Belfast, to Culdrose following modification work. A leaking fuel pipe caught fire after making contact with a hot exhaust, causing an extinguisher to explode, which severed more fuel lines. Whilst near Milton, the aircraft exploded, then crashed at Michael-on-Arrow, 15 miles west of Hereford, killing the pilot. XG890 was the only aircraft to see foreign service, being despatched direct to the West German Navy to serve as UA+99. Of the remainder, XG882 survives in a sorry state at Errol, XG883 is on loan from the FAA Museum to the Berkshire Air Museum, while parts of XG889 live on in XG882.

Production
Nine T.5s were ordered on 25 June 1954 under Contract 6/Acft/10545/CB.9(a), serialled XG882 to XG890. Only eight were built, as XG888 was produced as a T.2. XG890 was supplied to the West German Naval Air Arm as UA+99.

Technical data – Gannet T.5	
ENGINE	3,035ehp Double Mamba 101 (A.S.M.D.3)
WINGSPAN	54ft 4in
LENGTH	43ft
HEIGHT	13ft 8½in
EMPTY WEIGHT	14,069lb
LOADED WEIGHT	23,446lb
MAX SPEED	299mph
INITIAL CLIMB	2,000 ft/min
CEILING	25,000ft
RANGE	662 miles
ENDURANCE	4hrs 54mins at 150mph

Gannet T.5

The second production Gannet T.5, XG883, which first flew on 1 March 1957 and is on display today at the Berkshire Air Museum at Woodley. (Via Martyn Chorlton)

Gannet AS.4 (including COD.4 and ECM.6)

Design
The Gannet AS.4, its training variant, the T.5 and its sub-variants, the COD (Carrier-on-board).4, the ECM (Electronic Counter Measures).4 and Mk 6 all came about because of the rise in weight and the demands being placed upon the Gannet AS.1. More power was needed, and this was provided by the 3,035ehp Double Mamba 101 engine, which was first installed in ex-AS.1, WN372. After returning from hot weather trials at Idris, the aircraft re-emerged from the White Waltham factory as the prototype AS.4 and first flew in its new guise from Northolt on 12 March 1956.

The first production aircraft, XA412, quickly followed and, less than a month later, ex-AS.1s, XA410 and XA411. By July 1956, the prototype AS.4 had completed its hot weather trials, again at Idris, only weeks before the type entered operational service.

Six AS.4s were later converted to the COD.4, which was used as a VIP transport and very light cargo aircraft and, more importantly, to the crew of an aircraft carrier far out at sea, the mail. Further modifications saw the introduction of a handful of ECM variants. At least one aircraft became an ECM.4 fitted with NSM3009 ECM equipment, while six others were upgraded with a more powerful radar and updated electronics, with large pods under each wing to initially become the AS.6; these were later redesignated as ECM.6s.

Operational service
The Gannet AS.4 first entered service with 824 Squadron at Eglinton in August 1956, the type then went on to serve aboard HMS *Ark Royal* from January the following year. The AS.4 also joined 700, 810, 814, 815, 825, 847 and 849 squadrons, the last until May 1966, by which time the type had virtually been phased out. In the meantime though, 849 Squadron had been operating the Gannet COD.4 since September 1961, a type that served the unit until September 1974, only being surpassed by the T.5. The rare ECM variants only served in an operational capacity with 831 (Electronic Warfare) Squadron

Technical data – Gannet AS.4/6	
ENGINE	One 3,035ehp Double Mamba (A.S.M.D.3)
WINGSPAN	54ft 4in
LENGTH	43ft
HEIGHT	13ft 8½in
EMPTY WEIGHT	14,069lb
LOADED WEIGHT	23,446lb
MAX SPEED	299mph
INITIAL CLIMB	2,000 ft/min
CEILING	25,000ft
RANGE	662 miles
ENDURANCE	4hrs 54mins at 150mph

at Culdrose from February 1959 when the ECM.4 first arrived. Phased out by February 1961, the ECM.4 was superseded by the ECM.6, which arrived the same month and served until 16 May 1966, when the unit was disbanded at Watton and its personnel were moved to 360 Squadron.

Production

Eighty-two Gannet AS.4s were built, 58 of them at Hayes and 24 at Stockport. Six AS.4s were converted to COD.4s and nine to ECM.6 standard, which were originally designated as AS.6s (at least one aircraft, WN464, was converted to ECM.4 standard).

Fairey Gannet AS.4 XA425, captured by renowned aircraft photographer Charles E. Brown over east London on 15 August 1956. (Charles E. Brown via Martyn Chorlton)

XA454 was originally built as an AS.1, first flying in October 1956. After service with 814 Squadron aboard HMS *Eagle* and 849 Squadron at Culdrose, the aircraft was converted to a COD.4 in early 1963. In its new guise, the aircraft gave further excellent service until 1969 when it was struck off charge but spent the entire 1970s as Yeovilton's gate guard. (Via Martyn Chorlton)

Rotodyne

Development
The idea of producing a large commercially viable compound helicopter dated back to a study carried out in 1947 by Dr J. A. J. Bennett and Captain A. G. Forsyth. The project evolved through several different forms, the aircraft first being referred to as the Rotodyne in 1951. Two years later, the design settled on an aircraft that was to be powered by a pair of Napier Eland engines with tip jet propulsion.

Design
The unique Rotodyne was designed to carry up to 40 passengers with a flight crew of two, not including air hostesses/stewards. Beginning with its helicopter roots, the aircraft was fitted with a main rotor of 90ft in diameter, which was driven by tip jets fuel by compressed air and fuel via compressors fitted to the rear of the Eland engines. Both air and fuel were fed via the leading edge of the main plane up to the rotor head and then to opposing tip jets. Once a speed of 60mph was reached, the tip jets were extinguished, and the Eland engines took over while the 46ft 6in span main wing took over 50 per cent of the lift away from the rotor blades. This effectively turned the aircraft into a large high-speed autogyro in level flight. The rotor system was torque-less, so there was no need for the corrective tail rotor that is still traditional on helicopters today. To test all of the Rotodyne's systems fully before flight, test rigs were built at White Waltham and Boscombe Down. The latter incorporated a pair of Eland engines with propellers, a shorter version of the main plane and the entire rotor head with tip jets.

Service
Serialled XE521, the Rotodyne made its first untethered flight at White Waltham on 6 November 1957, in the hands of W. R. Gellatly and J. G. P. Morton, who were both destined to see the project through as the main flight test crew from start to finish. The same day, two further flights were carried out around the perimeter of the airfield. For the next five months, all flights were carried out as a helicopter, but, on 10 April 1958, the first transition from the hover was carried out at 4,000ft, an exercise that benefitted enormously from trials with the Jet Gyrodyne.

By late 1958, the performance of the Rotodyne was clearly good enough for an attempt on a speed record, and the most appropriate one, which reflected how the aircraft could be used, was the 100km (62 mile) closed-circuit category. On 5 January 1959, Gellatly and Morton, with Dr D. B. Leason (flight-test observer) and E. J. Blackburn (strain-gauge operator) in the back, flew a measured circuit between White Waltham and Hungerford. An average speed of 307km/h (190.9mph) was recorded, a speed 49mph faster than the previous straight line record set by a helicopter. This record stood until October 1961, when a Ka-22 Vintokryl convertiplane flew faster. Interest, by 1960, was growing across the world for the Rotodyne, especially from New York Airways, while one of the main intended recipients, BEA, began to go cool on the idea. However, the beginning of the end for the Rotodyne came on 8 February 1960, when Fairey Aviation and Westland Aircraft were merged. Westland was also soaking up Bristol's helicopter division as well, which resulted in the very protracted progress of the Rotodyne from the spring of 1960 onwards. Sadly, month by month through 1961, all interest in the aircraft began to dwindle, and with no sign of further government investment, the Rotodyne was cancelled in February 1962. Yet another great British design had been put out to grass.

Technical data – Rotodyne	
ENGINE	Two 2,800shp Napier Eland N.El.7 turboprops and four 1,000lb rotor-tip jets
WINGSPAN	46ft 6in
ROTOR DIAMETER	90ft
FUSELAGE LENGTH	58ft 8in
HEIGHT	22ft 2ins
INTERNAL CABIN LENGTH	46ft
LOADED WEIGHT	33,000lb
CRUISING SPEED	185mph
MAX RANGE	450 miles

The one and only Fairey Rotodyne, XE521, departing White Waltham on 29 August 1959 with Squadron Leader W. R. Gellatly at the controls. (Fairey via *Aeroplane*)

With the exception of the rotor revolutions, instruments and low-speed-range ASIs, the layout of the Rotodyne flight deck and panels were laid out as if the aircraft was a normal fixed-wing machine. (*Flight* via *Aeroplane*)

Gannet AEW.3

Development
The AEW (Airborne Early Warning) variant of the Gannet had been a long time coming for the Royal Navy, and, like the anti-submarine variant before it, an American-built type, the Skyraider AEW.1, had been brought in to fill the capability gap.

Design
While the AS.4 differed very little on the surface from the AS.1, there was no such confusion caused by the Gannet AEW.3. Below the fuselage was mounted a large radome, which concealed the aircraft's powerful AN/APS 20. The modification resulted in the aircraft's 3,875ehp Double Mamba 112 engine having to be moved forward so that the shorter exhausts or jet-pipes could be repositioned under the leading-edge wing root. The undercarriage was lengthened to clear the radome whilst on the ground, and the tail surfaces were also modified to a more angular design and increased area, complete with a high-aspect ratio rudder. Both the second and third cockpits were removed, while the interior of the fuselage was redesigned to accommodate a pair of radar operators, who accessed the aircraft via a new side entrance door. The prototype, XJ440, was first flown on 20 August 1958, with a radome fitted but carried no radar equipment, effectively being used as an aerodynamic test aircraft. Further trials were carried out aboard HMS *Centaur*, by which time the first production aircraft, XL449, made its maiden flight from Northolt on 2 December 1958.

Operational service
In August 1959, three Gannet AEW.3s were delivered to 700G Squadron, an Intensive Trials Unit based at Culdrose. On 1 February 1960, 700G was absorbed into 849 Squadron, the AEW.3 initially serving with 849A Flight. Even before the 849 Squadron takeover, the unit's AEW.3s had accumulated 1,855 flying hours between them, 1,300 of these between August and December 1959. 849 Squadron, which was divided into four separate flights, was the only unit destined to fly the AEW.3. The flights operated from five Royal Naval carriers over an 18-year period, beginning with 'C' Flight, which joined HMS *Hermes* in July 1960.

The main task of the AEW.3 at this time was to simply extend the range of the home aircraft carrier's line-of-sight range-protection system. The type was incredibly efficient at the task, many of the AEW.3s

Technical data – Gannet AEW.3	
ENGINE	One 3,875ehp Double Mamba 112 (A.S.M.D.8)
WINGSPAN	54ft 4in
LENGTH	44ft
HEIGHT	16ft 8in
LOADED WEIGHT	25,000lb
MAX SPEED	250mph
CEILING	25,000ft
RANGE	700 miles
ENDURANCE	5 to 6hrs at 130 to 140mph

in service achieving an average of 30 flying hours per month. During 1970, four AEW.3s joined HMS *Ark Royal*; the type eventually serving until December 1978 to become the last Fairey aircraft to serve operationally with the Royal Navy.

Production

Forty-four AEW.3s were built including the prototype, XJ440, followed by XL449 to XL456, XL471 to XL482, XL493 to XL503, XR431 to XR432, and XP197 to XP199, XP224 to XP229 and XR431 to XR433.

Right: The prototype Gannet AEW.3, XJ440, carried no radar and was only used for handling trials. Compared to earlier variants, the revised fin and rudder are evident. (Via Martyn Chorlton)

Below: Alongside XL449, Gannet AEW.3 XL451 was used for carrier deck trials on board HMS *Victorious* in May 1959. (Via Martyn Chorlton)

Fairey Numbers

A compilation of Fairey construction numbers, their serials (if applied) or registration, aircraft type and variant.

Below: A Fairey Firefly I returns to RNAS Ford after taking part in a Royal Navy/FAA exercise. (*Aeroplane*)

Key

Number in brackets after the type name is the number built.

First number in italics from 1-9516 is the aircraft's unique Fairey construction number.

Serial or registration runs from 3702-XR433.

Notes are in brackets with the following abbreviations: NB = Not Built; P = Prototype; A = Airframe only or used for spares, testing or development work; AF = built by Avions Fairey; NC = Not Completed; - = No serial applied; T = Trainer and RNNAS = Royal Netherlands Naval Air Service.

Fighter & F.2 Fighter (1) *1*, 3702(NB); *2*, 3704 (F.2); *3*, 3705, (NB)
Short 827 (12) *4-15*, 8550-8561
Campania (10) *16-25*, N1000-1009; *26*, -, (NB)
Sopwith 1½ Strutter (100) *27-126*, A954-1053
N.9/F.127 (1) *127*, N9/K-103/G-EAAJ/N-20
III (1) *128*, N10/G-EALQ, (P)
Hamble Baby (51) *129*, 8134, (P); *130-149*, N1320-1339; *150-179*, N1450-1479
Campania (40) *180-219*, N2360-2399
IIIA (50) *220-269*, N2850-2899
IIIB (5) *270-274*, N2225-2229
Atalanta (1) *275*, N118, (NC); *276*, N119
IIIB/C (30) *277-306*, N2230-2259
IIIC (30) *307-336*, N9230-9259
Titania (1) *337*, N129; *338*, -, (NB)
Pintail I, II, III (3) *339-341*, N133-135, (P)
N.3 FB (Flying-boat) (0) *342-343*, N88-89, (NB)
IIID (59) *344-393*, N9450-9499; *394-399*, ANA.1-6/A10.1-6, (Australia); *400-402*, -, (Portugal)
Fawn I/II (3) *403-405*, J6907-6909, (P)
Flycatcher (3) *406-408*, N163-165, (P)
III (Coastal Defence) (0) *409-410*, -, (NB)
IIID (4) *411*, -, (Portugal); *412-3*, -; *414*, -, (NC)
Fawn II (2) *415-6*, J6990-1, (P)
Flycatcher (3) *417-419*, N9611-9613, (D)
Fremantle (1) *420*, N173/G-EBLZ
IIID (12) *421-432*, N9567-9578
Flycatcher (6) *433-438*, N9614-9619
IIID (12) *439-450*, N9630-9641
Flycatcher (27) *451-476*, N9655-9680; *477*, N9697
Pintail IV (3) *478-480*, -, (Japan)
Fawn I (2) *481-2*, J7182-3
Fawn II (50) *483*, J7184; *484-5*, -, (A); *486-532*, J7185-7231
Spec 9/23 (Three-engine FB) (0) *533*, (NB)
Fawn II (2) *534-5*, -, (A)
III (Military Load Carrier) (0) *536*, -, (NB)
Fawn II (1) *537*, -, (A)
Ferret I, II, III (3) *538-540*, N190-192, (P)
Spec 26/23 (Single-engined day bomber) (0) *541*, (NB)
IIID (9) *542*,-, (Sweden); *543-549*, -, (Portugal); *550*, -, (NC)
III (GP Troop Carrier) (0) *551*, -, (NB)
IIID (20) *552-571*, N9730-9749
Firefly I (1) *572*, -, (P)
Fox I (1) *573*, J9515, (P)
IIIF (1) *574*, N198, (P)
IIID (2) *575*, - ; *576* (originally 439) G-EBKE, (British Guiana); *577*, -, (NB)
Flycatcher (36) *578-613*, N9854-9889
IIID (44) *614-655*, N9750-9791; *656-7*, - , (Mk IA, (NB))
Flycatcher (6) *658-663*, N9890-9895
IIID (6) *664-669*, -,
Flycatcher (24) *670-693*, N9902-9925
IIID (3) *694-5*, - , (Amphibian); *696*, - , (Sweden)
Flycatcher (40) *697-736*, N9926-9965
IIID (45) *737-772*, S1000-1035, (Mk II); *773-776*, F.1-4, (Netherlands); *777*, - , (Seaplane Trainer); *778* (Seaplane Trainer converted to day bomber); *779*, -, (Portugal); *780-1*, - , (A)
Single/two-seat fighter (0) *782*, -, (NB)
Fawn III (12) *783-794*, J7768-7779
IIID (3) *795-6*, -, (A); *797*, -
Flycatcher (14) *798-811*, S1060-1073
IIID (35) *812-846*, S1074-1108, (Mk III)
Fox I (18) *847-864*, J7941-7958
Fawn III (8) *865-872*, J7978-7985
Flycatcher II (1) *873*, N216
Felixstowe F.2A (Conversion) (1) *874*, -, (Portugal)
Fox I (5) *875-879*, J8423-8427 **IIIF** (11) *880-889*, S1139-1148; *890*, N225, (P)

Felixstowe F.2A (Conversion) (1) *891*, -, (Portugal)
IIIF (60) *892-906*, S1168-1182, (Mk I); *907-931*, S1183-1207, (Mk I); *932-951*, S1208-1227, (Mk II)
Fox I/IA (4) *952-955*, J9025-9028
IIIF (141) *956-967*, S1250-1261, (Mk II); *968*, S1262, (Mk II, Irish Free State); *969-975*, J9053-9059, (Mk IVC/M); *976-979, 23-26*, (Mk I, Chile); *980-997*, J9060-9077, (Mk IVC/M); *998-1020*, 19132-9154, (Mk IVC/M); *1021-1040*, J9155-9174, (Mk IVM); *1041-2*, -, (Mk IVM, [D]); *1043-1096*, S1303-1356, (Mk IIIM)
Flycatcher (25) *1097-1121*, S1273-1297
IIIF (7) *1122-1127*, AP-1-6, (Mk IIIM, Argentine); *1128*, -, (NB); *1129*, G-AABY/VH-UTT, (Mk IIIM)
Firefly II (1) *1130*, G-ABCN, (P)
L.R.M.1 (1) *1131*, J9479
Fleetwing (1) *1132*, N235
IIIF (4) *1133-4*, NZ631-2, (Mk IIIM, New Zealand); *1135-6*, -, (Mk IIIM, Irish Free State)
Firefly IIIM (1) *1137*, S1592/G-ABFH
Fox II (1) *1138*, J9834/G-ABFG, (P)
IIIF (132) *1139-1183*, J9637-9681, (Mk IVM/A); *1184-1231*, J9784-9831, (Mk IVM/A); *1232-1270*, S1370-1408, (Mk IIIM)
Hendon (1) *1271*, K1695, (P)
IIIF (1) *1272*, G-AASK, (Mk IIIM); *1273*, -, (Mk IIIM, [NB])
Flycatcher (11) *1274-1284*, S1409-1418
IIIF (111) *1285-1294*, S1454-1463, (Mk IIIM); *1295-1301*, K1115-1121, (Mk IIIM/A); *1302-1314*, K1158-1170, (Mk IIIM/A); *1315*, G-AATT, (Mk IIIM); *1316*, S1325, (Mk IIIM/Seal, [P]); *1317-1395*, S1474-1552, (Mk IIIB)
Gordon I (1) *1396*, K1697, (P)
IIIF/Gordon I (51) *1397-1427*, K1698-1728, (Mk IVB); *1428-1447*, K1729-1748
IIIF/Gordon I (41) *1448-1477*, K1749-1778, (Mk IVB/Gordon I); *1478*, -, (Mk IVM/A, Russia); *1479-1488*, -, (Mk IIIB, Greece)
Firefly (25) *1489-1513*, Y-1 to Y-25, (Belgium)
IIIF (1) *1514*, -, (Mk IIIB [Chile])
Gordon (1) *1515*, -, (China)
IIIF (66) *1516-1581*, S1779-1844, (Mk IIIB); *1582-3*, -, (Mk IVB [NB])
Gordon I (47) *1584-1630*, K2603-2649; *1631-1638*, -, (NB)
Fox II (12) *1639-1650*, 0-1 to 0-12, (Belgium)
Firefly II (20) *1651-1670*, A.F.5001-5020/Y-26 to Y-45, (AF)
L.R.M. II (1) *1671*, K1991
IIIF (21) *1672-1678*, S1845-1851, (Mk IIIB); *1679-1692*, S1852-1865, (Mk IIIB)
Firefly II (31) *1693-1722*; A.F.5021-5051, Y-46 to Y-75, (AF)
Fox II (31) *1723-1752*, A.F.6001-6030, (AF); *1753*, A.F.6031, (Fox VI [P][AF])
S.9/30 (1) *1754*, S1706
Gordon I (87) *1755-1802*, K2683-2730; *1803-1812*, -, (Brazil); *1813-1826*, K2731-2744; *1827-1836*, -, (Brazil); *1837-1841*, K2745-2749
Fox III/IV (1) *1842*, G-ABYY
Seal (32) *1843-1853*, K3477-3487; *1854-1874*, K3514-3534
TSR I (1) *1875*, -
Firefly II (1) *1876*, Among A.F.5022-5030, (Russia)
Gordon I (20) *1877-1896*, K2750-2769
Seal (16) *1897-1907*, K3535-3545; *1908-9*, K3575-6; *1910*, K3577, (Gordon II [P]); *1911-2*, K3578-9
Fox III (13) *1913-1925*, A.F.6033-6045, (AF)
G.4/31 (2) *1926*, K3905; *1927*, -, (NC)
Firefly II (6) *1928-1933*, A.F.5052-5057/Y-76 to Y-81, (AF)
Seal (6) *1934-1939*, -, (Peru)
Gordon II (24) *1940-1963*, K3986-4009
Fox Trainer & Fox II Floatplane (7) *1964*, A.F.6032/C-ACKH, (AF); *1965-1970*, -, (Peru)
Seal (25) *1971-1995*, K4201-4225
Fox III (36) *1996-2031*, A.F.6046-6081, (AF)
Firefly II (6) *2032-2037*, A.F.5058-5063/Y-82 to Y-87, (AF)
TSR II (1) *2038*, K4190
Fox VI (54) *2039-2092*, -, (AF)
Seal (25) *2093-2110*, K4779-4796; *2111*, -, (Argentina); *2112-2115*, -, (Latvia); *2116-7*, -, (Chile)
Fantome *2118*, F.6/G-ADIF, (P)
Fox VII (2) *2119*, A.F.6142, (AF); *2120*, A.F.6134, (AF)
Battle (1) *2121*, K4303, (P)

Seafox (2) *2122-3*, K4304-5, (P)
Hendon (14) *2124-2137*, K5085-5098; *2138-2141*, K5768-5771, (NB)
Swordfish I (89) *2142-2144*, K5660-5662, (D); *2145-2230*, K5926-6011
P.4/34 (1) *2231*, K5099, (P)
Fox VI (32) *2232-2241*, -, (AF); *2242-2245*, -, (AF); *2246-7*, 871-2/HB-HAF, -HAK (AF) (Switzerland); *2248-2263*, -, (AF)
Feroce (1) *2264-5*, -, (AF) (Russia)
P.4/34/Fulmar (1) *2266*, K7555, (P)
Seafox (49) *2267-2315*, K8569-8617
Battle (200) *2316-2470*, K7558-7712; *2471-2515*, K9176-9220
Fox IIIC (12) *2516-2527*, -, (AF)
Swordfish I (281) *2528-2631*, K8346-8449; *2632-2658*, K8860-8886; *2659-2808*, L2717-2866
Battle (465) *2809-3074*, K9221-9486; *3075-3121*, N2020-2066; *3122-3171*, N2082-2131; *3172-3215*, N2147-2190; *3216-3257*, N2211-2252; *3258-3273*, F.10-25, (Belgium)
Albacore (100) *3274-3373*, L7074-7173
Swordfish I (62) *3374-3403*, L7632-7661; *3404-3435*, L7670-7701
Seafox (15) *3436-3450*, L4519-4533
Fantome (1) *3451*, L7045, (AF)
Battle (6) *3452-3457*, N2253-2258
Swordfish I (60) *3458-3487*, L9714-9743; *3488-3517*, L9756-9785
Albacore (189) *3518-3566*, N4152-4200; *3567-3616*, N4219-4268; *3617-3666*, N4281-4330; *3667-3706*, N4347-4386
Fulmar I (250) *3707-3746*, N1854 (G-AIBE)-1893; *3747-3796*, N1910-1959; *3797-3833*, N1980-2016; *3834-3883*, N3994-4043; *3884-3924*, N4060-4100; *3925-3956*, N4116-4147
Albacore (11) *3957-3961*, N4387-4391; *3962-3967*, N4420-4425
Battle (250) *3968-3997*, P6480-6509; *3998-4047*, P6523-6572; *4048-4067*, P6596-6615; *4068-4117*, P2155-2204; *4118-4163*, P2223-2278; *4164-4200*, P2300-2336; *4201-4217*, P2353-2369
Swordfish I (200) *4218-4266*, P3991-4039; *4267-4301*, P4061-4095; *4302-4348*, P4123-4169; *4349-4390*, P4191-4232; *4391-4417*, P4253-4279
Battle (152) *4418-4442*, P5228-5252; *4443-4467*, P5270-5284; *4468-9*, P1767, 1770, (P); *4470-4499*, P6616-6645, (T); *4500-4529*, P6663-6692, (T); *4530-4549*, P6718-6737, (T); *4550-4569*, P6750-6769, (T)
Barracuda I (25) *4570-4594*, P9642-9666
Barracuda II (225) *4595-4619*, P9667-9691; *4620-4659*, P9709-9748; *4660-4709*, P9787-9836; *4710-4754*, P9847-9891; *4755-4789*, P9909-9943; *4790-4819*, P9957-9986
Battle T (100) *4820-4849*, R7356-7385; *4850-4899*, R7399-7448; *4900-4919*, R7461-7480
Albacore (100) *4920-4964*, T9131-9175; *4965-4989*, T9191-9215; *4990-5019*, T9231-9260
Fulmar II (200) *5020-5069*, X8525-8574; *5070-5114*, X8611-8655; *5115-5149*, X8680-8714; *5150-5199*, X8729-8778; *5200-5219*, X8798-8817
Albacore (250) *5220-5264*, X8940-8984; *5265-5314*, X9010-9059; *5315-5359*, X9073-9117; *5360-5409*, X9137-9186; *5410-5429*, X9214-9233; *5430-5469*, X9251-9290
Firefly I (198) *5470-5473*, Z1826-1829, (P); *5474-5489*, Z1830-1845; *5490-5539*, Z1865-1914; *5540-5584*, Z1942-1986; *5585-5632*, Z2011-2058; *5633-5638*, TW677-682 (three NB); *5639-5663*, Z2096-2120; *5664-5667*, TW683-686, (NB)
Firefly 4 (2) *5668-9*, TW687-688
Albacore (150) *5670-5704*, BF584-618; *5705-5754*, BF631-680; *5755-5799*, BF695-739; *5800-5819*, BF758-777
Fulmar II (150) *5820-5841*, BP775-796; *5842-5869*, BP812-839; *5870-5919*, DR633-682; *5920-5969*, DR700-749
Barracuda II (50) *5970-5988*, DT813-831; *5989-6009*, DT845-865; *6010-6019*, DT878-887
Firefly 4 (5) *6020-6024*, TW689-693
Firefly I (19) *6025-6043*, DT931-949
Firefly 4 (12) *6044-6049*, TW694-699; *6050-6055*, TW715-720

Firefly I (18) *6056-6073*, DT974-991
Firefly 4 (12) *6074-6085*, TW721-732
Firefly I (18) *6086-6103*, DV117-134
Firefly 4 (12) *6104-6115*, TW733-744
Firefly I (203) *6116-6119*, DV147-150;
6120-6165, PP391-436; *6166*, PP437/F-3, (RNNAS); *6167-8*, PP456-457; *6169*, PP458/F-1, (RNNAS); *6170-6182*, PP459-471; *6183*, PP472/F-2, (RNNAS); *6184*, PP473; *6185*, PP474/F-10, (RNNAS); *6186-6194*, PP475-483; *6195*, PP484/F-6, (RNNAS); *6196*, PP485; *6197-8*, PP486-7/F-7, F-5, (RNNAS); *6199*, PP488; *6200*, PP489/F-4 (RNNAS); *6201-2*, PP490-491; *6203*, PP492/F-8, (RNNAS); *6204-5*, PP493-4/F-9, F-14, (RNNAS); *6206-7*, PP495-6; *6208*, PP497/F-12, (RNNAS); *6209-6211*, PP523-525; *6213-6214*, PP526-528/F-15, -11,-13 (RNNAS); *6215-6253*, PP529-567; *6254-6256*, PP580-582; *6257*, PP583/F-16, (RNNAS); *6258-6263*, PP584-589; *6264-6267*, PP590-593/F-17 to -20, (RNNAS); *6268-6274*, PP594-600; *6275-6277*, PP601-603/F-21 to -23, (RNNAS); *6278-9*, PP604-5; *6280-1*, PP606-7/F-24 and 25, (RNNAS); *6282-6287*, PP608-613; *6288-6290*, PP614-616/F-26 to -28, (RNNAS); *6291-2*, PP617-8; *6293*, PP619/F-29, (RNNAS); *6294-6296*, PP620-622; *6297*, PP623/F-30, (RNNAS); *6298-6319*, PP639-660
Barracuda II (428) *6320-6362*, LS464-506; *6363-6400*, LS519-556; *6401-6428*, LS568-595; *6429-6435*, LS596-602; *6436-6474*, LS615-653; *6475-6520*, LS668-713; *6521-6558*, LS726-763; *6559-6601*, LS778-820; *6602-6647*, LS833-878; *6648-6693*, LS891-936; *6694-6719*, LS949-974
Barracuda III (460) *6720-6761*, PM682-723; *6762-6804*, PM738-780; *6805-6847*, PM796-838; *6848-6893*, PM852-897; *6894-6939*, PM913-958 (Mk V [P]); *6940-6969*, PM970-999; *6970-7019*, PN115-164; *7020-7061*, RK328-369; *7062-7108*, RK382-428; *7109-7153*, RK441-485; *7154-7179*, RK498-523
Barracuda V (30) *7180-7192*, RK530-542; *7193-7209*, RK558-574; *7210-7369*, Within RK575-784, (NB)
Firefly I (59) *7370-7411*, MB378-419; *7412-7428*, MB433-449

Firefly 4 (10) *7429-7438*, TW745-754
Firefly I (430) *7439-7458*, MB460-479; *7459-7503*, MB492-536; *7504-7548*, MB549-593; *7549-7585*, MB613-649; *7586-7627*, MB662-703; *7628-7669*, MB717-758; *7670-7718*, DK414-462, (General Aircraft); *7719-7756*, DK476-513, (General Aircraft); *7757-7801*, DK526-570 (General Aircraft); *7802-7833*, DK588-619, (NB); *7834-7869*, DK632-667, (NB)
Spearfish (5) *7870*, RA356, (P); *7871*, RA360, (P); *7872*, RA363, (P); *7873*, RN241, (P); *7874*, TJ175, (NC); *7875-6*, TJ179, TJ184, (NB); *7877-7976*, - , (NB)
Firefly FR.4 (67) *7977-8019*, VG957-999; *8020-8043*, VH121-144; *8044-8176*, Within VH145-361, (N.F.4 [NB])
Spearfish (0) *8177-8197*, TS915-935, (NB); *8198-8225*, TS963-990, (NB); *8226*, TT110, (NB)
Firefly FR.4 (40) *8227-8266*, 11-31 to -70/16-31 to -70, (RNNAS)
Spec N.16/45 (Strike Aircraft) (0) *8267-8269*, - , (NB)
Gannet (2) *8270-1*, VR546, VR557, (P)
Firefly FR.4 (70) *8272-8291*, VT362-381; *8292-8341*, VT392-441
Firefly FR.4/5 (47) *8342-8388*, VT458-504
Firefly NF.5 (14) *8389-8402*, 11-71 to -84/16-71 to -84, (RNNAS)
Firefly FR.4/5 (52) *8403-8428*, VX371-396; *8429-8454*, VX413-438
Primer (2) *8455-6*, G-ALBL, G-ALEW; *8457-8464*, - , (NB)
Gyrodyne (1) *8465*, VX591/G-AIKF
F.D.1 (1) *8466*, VX350; *8467-8*, VX357, VX364, (NB)
Firefly 5 (169) *8469-8498*, WB243-272; *8499-8534*, WB281-316; *8535-8587*, WB330-382; *8588-8637*, WB391-440
Firefly 5/6 (6) *8638-8643*, WB505-510
Firefly 6 (105) *8644-8651*, WB516-523; *8652-8700*; WD824-872; *8701-8748*, WD878-925
Gannet (1) *8749*, WE488, (P)
Firefly 6 (6) *8750-8755*, WH627-632
Firefly AS.7 (52) *8756-8784*, WJ146-174; *8785-8807*, WJ187-209

Firefly AS.6 (18) *8808-8825*, WJ104-121
Firefly 7 (2) *8826-7*, WJ215-6, (D)
Firefly AS.7 (45) *8828-8853*, WK348-373; *8854-8872* (19), WM761-779
Firefly AS.7/U.8 (82) *8873-8909*, WM796-832; *8910-8954*, WM855-899
Firefly U.8 (4) *8955-8958*, WP351-354
Firefly AS.7 (0) *8959-9059*, Within WP355-490, (NB); *9060-9084*, WV967-991, (NB); *9085-9110*, WW103-128, (NB)
Gannet AS.1 (26) *9111-9136*, WN339-364
Gannet T.2 (1) *9137*, WN365, (P)
Gannet AS.1 (142) *9138-9150*, WN366-378; *9151-9190*, WN390-429; *9191-9210*, WN445-464; *9211-9256*, XA319-364; *9257-9279*, XA387-409
Gannet AS.4 (24) *9280-9303*, XA410-433
Gannet AS.1 (1) *9304*, XA434
Gannet AS.4 (1) *9305*, XA435
Gannet AS.1 (1) *9306*, XA436
Gannet AS.4 (20) *9307-9326*, XA454-473
Gannet AS.1 (1) *9327*, XD898
Gannet T.2 (23) *9328-9350*, XA508-530
Gannet AS.1/4 (16) *9351-9366*, XG783-798
Gannet AS.1 (2) *9367-8*, XG825-6
Gannet AS.4 (29) *9369-9397*, XG827-855
Gannet T.2 (13) *9398-9410*, XG869-881
Gannet T.5 (6) *9411-9416*, XG882-887
Gannet T.2 (1) *9417*, XG888
Gannet T.5 (2) *9418-9*, XG889-890
Gyrodyne/Jet Gyrodyne (1) *9420*, G-AJJP/XJ389
F.D.2 (2) *9421-2*, WG774, WG777
Ultra-light Helicopter *9423*, XJ924; *9424*, XJ928/G-AOUJ; *9425*, XJ930; *9426*, XJ936/G-AOUK; *9427*, -; *9428*, G-APJJ
Rotodyne (1) *9429*, XE521, ('V'); *9430*, XH249, ('Z') (NB)
Gannet AEW.3 (41) *9431*, XJ440, (P); *9432-9471*, XL449-456, XL471-482, 493-503, XP197-199, 224-229
Westland Scout (40) *9472-9483*, XP846-857; *9484-9511*, XP883-910
Gannet AS.4 (2) *9512-3*, -
Gannet AEW.3 (3) *9514-9516*, XR431-433

Fairey received an order to build 100 Sopwith 1½ Strutters in mid-1916. Work began in October 1916 at the company's Clayton Road factory and was completed by September 1917. (Via Martyn Chorlton)

Fairey – the subcontract work

From its inception and through to its merger with Westland Aviation, Fairey produced aircraft for other aircraft companies including Short Brothers, Bristol, Handley Page and de Havilland.

Short Type 827
8550-8561 (c/n 4-15)
Total: 12

Sopwith 1½ Strutter
A954-1053 (c/n 27-126)
Total: 100

Felixstowe F.2A (Conversion for Portugal)
C/n 874 & 891
Total: 2

Bristol Beaufighter IC & IF
337 Beaufighter IFs and ICs were delivered between February 1941 and April 1942 by Fairey, Heaton Chapel to Contract No. B41906/39. T4623-4649 were built as IFs. T4623-4647, T4648-4670, 4700-4734, 4751-4800, 4823-4836, 4862-4899, 4915-4947, 4970-5007, 5027-5055 and 5070-5099

Bristol Beaufighter VI
163 Beaufighter VIs were delivered between April 1942 and May 1943 by Fairey, Heaton Chapel to Contract No. B41906/39. T5100-5114, 5130-5175, 5195-5220, 5250-5299 and 5315-5352

Handley Page Halifax V
150 Halifax Vs were delivered between October 1942 and August 1943 by Fairey Aviation, Stockport. DJ980-999, DK114-151, 165-207 and 223-271

Handley Page Halifax V
96 Halifax Vs were delivered between August 1943 and January 1944 by Fairey Aviation, Stockport. LK626-667, 680-711 and 725-746

Handley Page Halifax III
104 Halifax IIIs were delivered between January and April 1944 by Fairey Aviation, Stockport. LK747-766, 779-812, 826-850 and 863-887

Handley Page Halifax B.III
180 Halifax IIIs were delivered between April and November 1944 by Fairey Aviation, Ringway. NA492-531, 543-587, 599-644 and 656-704

Handley Page Halifax III
41 Halifax IIIs were delivered between October 1944 and February 1945 by Fairey Aviation, Stockport. PN167-207

Handley Page Halifax A.VII/B.VII
90 Halifax VIIs were delivered between February and October 1945 by Fairey Aviation, Stockport. PN208, PN223-267, 285-327 and 343 (PN345-362, RS227-497, TM944-TN247, totalling 368 Halifaxes, were all cancelled)

De Havilland Vampire FB.9
51 Vampire FB.9s were built by Fairey Aviation, Stockport, to Contract No. 6/Acft/6422. WR205-215 and 230-269

Westland Scout AH.1
40 Scout AH.1s produced for the Army Air Corps to Contract KF/2Q/06. XP846-857 and XP883-910

Right: The award from Short Brothers for a dozen Type 827 reconnaissance floatplanes was the company's first order and was clearly influenced by Charles Richard Fairey's close association with the Rochester-based company. (Via Martyn Chorlton)

Below: Fairey built 320 Beaufighter ICs at its Heaton Chapel factory in Stockport, including T4638, pictured serving with 604 (County of Middlesex) Squadron. (Via Martyn Chorlton)

Stockport-built Halifax GR.V, LK688, of 202 Squadron, one of 246 built by Fairey, between October 1942 and January 1944. (Via Martyn Chorlton)

Fairey built 325 Halifax IIIs at Stockport and Ringway between January 1944 and February 1945. (Via Martyn Chorlton)

The final batch of Fairey-built Halifaxes were Mk VIIs, all built at Stockport and delivered between February and October 1945. Many were converted to transport C.VII standard, including PN261, seen here serving with 298 Squadron. (Via Martyn Chorlton)

Vampire FB.9 WR266, one of 51 built by Fairey at Stockport, which were all delivered to the RAF by late 1952. (Via Martyn Chorlton)

Above: Although Fairey had been merged with Westland by this time, the company was still credited with the production of 40 Scout AH.1s, including this aircraft, XP884. (Via Martyn Chorlton)

Right: Fairey aircraft will be forever associated with their service with the Royal Navy, which lasted from World War One through to the late 1970s. One of the most iconic was undoubtedly the Fairey Swordfish from whose rear cockpit this photograph was taken of HMS *Ocean* in October 1945. This was the very last flight of a Swordfish from the deck of a Royal Navy aircraft carrier. (*Aeroplane*)

Other books you might like:

Historic Military Aircraft Series, Vol. 1

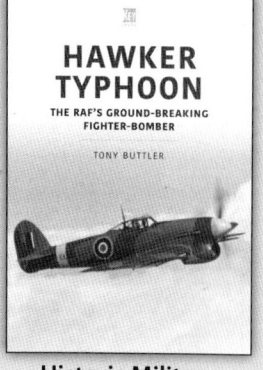
Historic Commercial Aircraft Series, Vol. 6

Historic Military Aircraft Series, Vol. 7

Historic Military Aircraft Series, Vol. 5

For our full range of titles please visit:
shop.keypublishing.com/books

VIP Book Club

Sign up today and receive
TWO FREE E-BOOKS

Be the first to find out about our forthcoming book releases and receive exclusive offers.

Register now at **keypublishing.com/vip-book-club**

Our VIP Book Club is a 100% spam-free zone, and we will never share your email with anyone else. You can read our full privacy policy at: privacy.keypublishing.com